Dictionary
of
First Names

BROCKHAMPTON PRESS

This edition published 1995 by Brockhampton Press,
a member of Hodder Headline PLC.

ISBN 1 86019 008 1

Printed and bound in Slovenia

A

Aaron *masc* mountaineer, enlightener (*Hebrew*); a contracted dimunitive is **Arn**.

Abbie, Abby *fem* diminutive *forms* of **Abigail**, also used independently.

Abbott *masc* a surname, meaning father of the abbey, used as a first name (*Old English*).

Abe *masc* father (*Aramaic*); diminutive of **Abraham, Abram**.

Abel *masc* breath, fickleness, vanity (*Hebrew*).

Abelard *masc* nobly resolute (*Germanic*).

Abiathar *masc* father of plenty or excellence (*Hebrew*).

Aberah *fem* a variant form of **Averah**.

Abiel *masc* father of strength (*Hebrew*).

Abigail *fem* my father's joy (*Hebrew*); diminutive forms are **Abbie, Abby, Gail**.

Abihu *masc* to whom Jehovah is a father (*Hebrew*).

Abijah *masc* to whom Jehovah is a father (*Hebrew*); a diminutive form is **Bije**.

Abner *masc* father of light (*Hebrew*).

Abra *fem* mother of multitudes (*Hebrew*).

Abraham *masc* father of a multitude (*Hebrew*);
   diminutive forms are **Abe, Bram**.

Abram *masc* father of elevation (*Hebrew*); diminutive
   forms are **Abe, Bram**.

Absalom *masc* my father is peace (*Hebrew*).

Acacia *fem* the name of a plant, possibly meaning
   immortality and resurrection, used as a first name
   (*Greek*).

Acantha *fem* thorny, spiney (*Greek*).

Ace *masc* unity, unit (*Latin*).

Ackerley *masc* a surname, meaning from the acre
   meadow, used as a first name (*Old English*).

Ackley *masc* a surname, meaning from the oak tree
   meadow, used as a first name (*Old English*).

Ada *fem* diminutive of **Adela** or names beginning with
   Adal, also used independently; a variant form of
   Adah.

Adabelle *fem* joyful and beautiful, a combination of
   Ada and **Belle**; variant forms are **Adabel, Adabela,
   Adabella**.

Adah *fem* ornament (*Hebrew*); a variant form is **Ada**.

Adair *masc* a Scottish form of **Edgar**.

Adalard *masc* noble and brave (*Germanic*).

Adalia *fem* an early Saxon tribal name whose origin is
   unknown (*Germanic*).

Adam *masc* man, earth man, red earth (*Hebrew*).

Adamina *fem* of Adam (*Latin*).

Adar *fem* fire; as the name in the Jewish calendar for the twelfth month of the Biblical year and the sixth month of the civil year, it is a name sometimes given to girls born in that period (*Hebrew*).

Addie *fem* diminutive of **Adelaide**.

Addie, Addy, Mina.

Addison *masc* a surname, meaning Adam's son, used as a first name (*Old English*).

Adela *fem* of noble birth; a princess (*Germanic*).

Adelaide *fem* of noble birth; a princess (*Germanic*); a diminutive form is **Addie**.

Adelbert *see* **Albert**.

Adèle, Adele *fem* the French form of Adela, now also used as an English form.

Adelheid *fem* noble kind (*Germanic*); a diminutive form is **Heidi**.

Adeline, Adelina *fem* of noble birth; a princess (*Germanic*); a diminutive form is **Aline**.

Adelphia *fem* sisterly, eternal friend of mankind (*Greek*); variant forms are **Adelfia, Adelpha**.

Adin *masc* sensual (*Hebrew*).

Adina *fem* voluptuous, ripe, mature (*Hebrew*).

Adlai *masc* God is just (*Hebrew*).

Adler *masc* eagle, perceptive one (*Germanic*).

Adney *masc* island-dweller (*Old English*).

Adolf *masc* the German form of **Adolph**.

Adolph, Adolphus *masc* noble wolf; noble hero

(*Germanic*); a diminutive form is **Dolph**.

Adolpha *fem* noble she-wolf, she who will give her life for her young, the *fem* form of Adolf (*Germanic*); variant forms are **Adolfa, Adolfina, Adolphina**.

Adolphe *masc* the French form of **Adolph**.

Adon, Adonai *masc* lord, a sacred word for God (*Hebrew*).

Adonia *fem* beautiful goddess of the resurrection; eternal renewal of youth (*Greek*).

Adoniram *masc* lord of height (*Hebrew*).

Adora *fem* adored and beloved gift (*Latin*).

Adorabella *fem* beautiful gift, a combination of **Adora** and **Bella**.

Adorna *fem* adorned with jewels (*Latin*).

Adrian *masc* of the Adriatic in Italy (*Latin*); a variant form is **Hadrian**.

Adrianne, Adrienne *fem* forms of **Adrian**.

Adriel *masc* from God's congregation (*Hebrew*).

Aefa *fem* a variant form of **Aoife**.

Aeneas *masc* commended (*Greek*); a variant form is **Eneas**.

Aethelbert *see* **Ethelbert**.

Aethelred *see* **Ethelred**.

Afonso *masc* the Portugese form of **Alphonso**.

Afra *fem* a variant form of **Aphra**.

Africa *fem* the name of the continent used as a first name.

Agatha *fem* good; kind (*Greek*); a diminutive form is
    Aggie, Aggy.

Agave *fem* illustrious, famous (*Greek*).

Aggie, Aggy *fem* diminutive forms of **Agatha, Agnes**.

Agnes *fem* chaste; pure (*Greek*); diminutive forms are
    Aggie, Aggy, Agneta, Nessa, Nessie.

Agnès *fem* the French form of **Agnes**.

Agnese *fem* the Italian form of **Agnes**.

Agostino *masc* the Italian form of **Augustine**.

Agustín *masc* the Spanish form of **Augustine**.

Ahern *masc* horse lord, horse owner (*Irish Gaelic*).

Ahren *masc* eagle (*Germanic*).

Aidan *masc* fire, flame (*Irish Gaelic*); a variant form is
    Edan.

Aiken *masc* the Scottish form of **Atkin**, a surname
    meaning son of Adam, used as a first name (*Old
    English*).

Ailean *fem* Scots Gaelic form of **Alan**.

Aileen *fem* a variant form of **Eileen**.

Ailsa *fem* fairy (*Scots Gaelic*).

Aimée *fem* the French form of **Amy**.

Áine *fem* an Irish Gaelic form of **Anna**.

Ainsley *masc* a surname, meaning meadow of the
    respected one, used as a first name (*Old English*).

Ainslie *masc* a Scottish form of **Ainsley**, used as a first
    name.

Aisleen, Aisling *fem* vision (*Irish Gaelic*).

Al *masc* diminutive of **Alan, Albert**, etc.

Alain *masc* the French form of **Alan**.

Alan *masc* meaning uncertain, possibly a hound (*Slavonic*), harmony (*Celtic*); variant forms are **Allan, Allen**.

Alana, Alanna, Alannah *fem* forms of **Alan**; a variant form is **Lana**.

Alard *masc* a variant form of **Allard**.

Alaric *masc* noble ruler; all-rich (*Germanic*).

Alarice *fem* of **Alaric** (*Germanic*); variant forms are **Alarica, Alarise**.

Alasdair, Alastair *masc* variant forms of **Alister**.

Alban *masc* white, or of Alba in Italy (*Latin*).

Albern *masc* noble warrior (*Old English*).

Albert *masc* all-bright; illustrious (*Germanic*); diminutive forms are **Al, Bert, Bertie**.

Alberta *fem* form of **Albert**.

Albin *see* **Alban**.

Albina *fem* white, very fair (*Latin*);.variant forms are **Albinia, Alvina, Aubina, Aubine**.

Albrecht *masc* a German form of **Albert**.

Alcina *fem* strong-minded one, from a legendary woman who could make gold from stardust (*Greek*).

Alcott *masc* the surname, meaning old cottage or hut, used as a first name (*Old English*).

Alcyone *fem* in Greek mythology a woman who drowned herself from grief at her husband's death and

who was turned into a kingfisher; variant forms are
Halcyone, Halcyon.

Alda *fem* wise and rich (*Germanic*); variant forms are
Eada, Elda.

Alden *masc* a surname, meaning old or trustworthy
friend, used as a first name (*Old English*).

Alder *masc* a surname, meaning alder tree, used as a
first name (*Old English*); old, wise and rich (*Germanic*).

Aldis *masc* a surname, meaning old house, used as a
first name (*Old English*); *fem* a diminutive of some
names beginning with *Ald-*.

Aldo, Aldous *masc* old (*Germanic*).

Aldora *fem* of noble rank (*Old English*); variant forms
are **Aelda, Aeldra**.

Aldrich *masc* a surname, meaning old, wise ruler, used
as a first name (*Old English*).

Aldwin *see* **Alvin**.

Alec, Aleck *masc* diminutive *forms* of **Alexander**.

Aled *masc* the name of a river used as a first name
(*Welsh*).

Aleria *fem* like an eagle (*Latin*).

Aleron *masc* eagle (*Latin*).

Alethea *fem* truth (*Greek*).

Alex *masc* diminutive of **Alexander**; *fem* diminutive of
Alexandra, now both used independently; a variant
form is **Alix**.

Alexa *fem* diminutive of **Alexandra**.

Alexander *masc* a helper of men (*Greek*); diminutive forms are **Alec, Alex, Alick, Lex, Sandy.**

Alexandra, Alexandrina *fem* forms of **Alexander**; diminutive forms are **Alex, Alexa, Lexie, Lexy, Sandie, Sandra, Sandy.**

Alexia *fem* form of **Alexis**.

Alexina *fem* form of **Alexander**.

Alexis *masc fem* help; defence (*Greek*).

Alf, Alfie *masc* diminutive forms of **Alfred**.

Alfonsine *fem* form of **Alphonse** (*Germanic*); variant forms are **Alphonsina, Alphonsine, Alphonza**.

Alfonso *masc* a Spanish and Italian form of **Alphonso**.

Alford *masc* a surname, meaning old ford, used as a first name (*Old English*).

Alfred *masc* good or wise counsellor (*Germanic*); diminutive forms are **Alf, Alfie**.

Alfreda *fem* form of **Alfred**; diminutive forms are **Alfie, Allie**; variant forms are **Elfreda, Elfreida, Elfrieda, Elfrida, Elva, Elga, Freda**.

Alger *masc* elf spear (*Old English*).

Algernon *masc* whiskered (*Old French*); a diminutive form is **Algie, Algy**.

Alice, Alicia *fem* of noble birth; a princess (*Germanic*).—variant forms are **Alys, Alyssa**.

Alick *masc* diminutive of **Alexander**, now sometimes used independently.

Alida *fem* little bird; small and lithe (*Latin*); a Hungarian form of **Adelaide**; variant forms are **Aleda, Aleta, Alita**; diminutive forms are **Leda, Lita**.

Aliénor *fem* a French form of **Eleanor**.

Alima *fem* learned in music and dancing (*Arabic*).

Aline *fem* a contraction of **Adeline**.

Alison *fem* diminutive of **Alice**, now used entirely in its own right; a variant form is **Allison**; diminutive forms are **Allie, Ally**; *masc* son of Alice; son of a nobleman (*Old English*).

Alister *masc* the Scots Gaelic form of **Alexander**; variant forms are **Alasdair, Alastair**.

Alix *fem* a variant form of **Alex**.

Allan, Allen *masc* variant forms of **Alan**.

Allard *masc* noble and brave (*Old English*)*;* a variant form is **Alard,**

Allegra *fem* a word for cheerful or blithe used as a first name (*Italian*).

Allie, Ally *fem* diminutive of **Alice, Alison**.

Allison *fem* a variant form of **Alison**.

Allison, Al, Allie.

Alloula, Allula, Aloula.

Alma *fem* loving, nurturing (*Latin*).

Almira *fem* lofty; a princess (*Arabic*).

Almo *masc* noble and famous (*Old English*).

Aloha *fem* a word for welcome used as a first name (*Hawaiian*).

Alonso *masc* a Spanish form of **Alphonso**; a diminutive form is **Lonnie**.

Alonzo *see* **Alphonso**.

Aloysius *masc* a Latin form of **Lewis**.

Alpha *masc, fem* first one (*Greek*).

Alpheus *masc* exchange (*Hebrew*).

Alphonse *masc* the French form of **Alphonso**.

Alphonso, Alphonsus *masc* all-ready; willing (*Old German*).

Alpin *masc* blond (*Scottish Gaelic*).

Alroy *masc* red-haired (*Scottish Gaelic*).

Alston *masc* a surname, meaning old stone, used as a first name (*Old English*).

Alta *fem* tall in spirit (*Latin*).

Althea *fem* a healer (*Greek*); a diminutive form is **Thea**.

Altman *masc* old, wise man (*Germanic*).

Alton *masc* a surname, meaning old stream or source, used as a first name (*Old English*).

Alula *fem* winged one (*Latin*); first (*Arabic*).

Alun *masc* the Welsh form of **Alan**.

Alura *fem* divine counsellor (*Old English*).

Alva *fem* white (*Latin*).

Alva *see* **Alban**.

Alvah *masc* exalted one (*Hebrew*).

Alvin, Alwin *masc* winning all (*Old English*).

Alvina, Alvine *fem* beloved and noble friend (*Ger-*

manic); a diminutive form is **Vina**.

Alys, Alyssa *fem* variant forms of **Alice, Alicia**.

Alyth *fem* a placename, meaning steep place, used as a first name.

Alzena *fem* woman, purveyor of charm and virtue (*Arabic*).

Amabel *fem* lovable (*Latin*); a diminutive form is **Mabel**.

Amadea *fem* form of **Amadeus**.

Amadeus *masc* lover of God (*Latin*).

Amado *masc* the Spanish form of **Amato**.

Amalia *fem* work (*Germanic*); an Italian and Greek form of **Amelia**.

Amanda *fem* worthy of love (*Latin*); diminutive forms are **Manda, Mandy**.

Amariah *masc* whom Jehovah promised (*Hebrew*).

Amasa *masc* a burden (*Hebrew*).

Amber *fem* the name of a gemstone used as a first name.

Ambert *masc* shining bright light (*Germanic*).

Ambrogio *masc* the Italian form of **Ambrose**.

Ambrose *masc* immortal (Greek).

Ambrosine *fem* form of Ambrose; variant forms are **Ambrosia, Ambrosina**.

Amédée *masc* the French form of **Amadeus**.

Amelia *fem* busy, energetic (*Germanic*); a diminutive form is **Millie**.

Amélie *fem* the French form of **Amelia**.

Amelinda *fem* beloved and pretty (*Spanish*); variant forms are **Amalinda, Amelinde**.

Amena *fem* honest, truthful (*Gaelic*).

Amerigo *masc* an Italian variant form of **Enrico**.

Amery *masc* a variant form of **Amory**.

Amethyst *fem* the name of the semi-precious gemstone used as a first name (*Greek*).

Aminta, Amintha, Aminthe *fem* protector, a shepherdess in Greek mythology (*Greek*).

Ammon *masc* hidden (*Egyptian*).

Amory *masc* famous ruler (*Germanic*); variant forms are **Amery, Emery, Emmery**.

Amos *masc* bearer of a burden (*Hebrew*).

Amy *fem* beloved (*Old French*).

Anastasia *fem* rising up, resurrection (*Greek*); diminutive forms are **Stacey, Stacy, Stacie, Stasia**.

Anastasius *masc* form of **Anastasia**.

Anatholia, Anatola *fem* forms of Anatole (*Greek*; a variant form is **Anatolia**.

Anatole *masc* from the East (*Greek*).

Anatolia *fem* a variant form of **Anatholia**.

Andie *masc* diminutive of **Andrew**.

André *masc* the French form of **Andrew**, becoming popular as an English-language form.

Andrea *fem* form of **Andreas** or **Andrew**; a variant form is **Andrina**; *masc* the Italian form of **Andrew**.

Andreas *masc* Greek, Latin, and German forms of
   Andrew.

Andrés *masc* the Spanish form of **Andrew**.

Andrew *masc* strong; manly; courageous (*Greek*);
   diminutive forms are **Andie, Andy, Dandie, Drew**.

Andrina, Andrine *fem* variant forms of **Andrea**.

Aneirin, Aneurin *masc* noble, modest (*Welsh*); a
   diminutive form is **Nye**.

Anemone *fem* windflower, the name of the garden plant
   used as a first name (*Greek*).

Angel *fem* diminutive of **Angela** (*Greek*); *masc* form of
   Angela.

Angela, Angelina messenger (*Greek*).

Angelica *fem* lovely; angelic (*Greek*).

Angelo *masc* Italian form of **Angel**.

Angharad *fem* much loved (*Welsh*).

Angus *masc* excellent virtue (*Gaelic*); a diminutive
   form is **Gus**.

Anita *fem* Spanish diminutive of **Ann**, now used
   independently as an English-language form; a
   diminutive form is **Nita**.

Ann *fem* grace (*Hebrew*); a variant form is **Hannah**; a
   diminutive form is **Annie**.

Anna *fem* the Latin form of **Ann**.

Annabel, Annabelle, Annabella *fem* lovable (possibly
   from **Amabel**); diminutive forms are **Bella, Belle**.

Annan *masc* a Scottish placename, meaning water or

waters, used as a first name (*Scottish Gaelic*).

Anne *fem* the French form of **Ann**.

Anneka *fem* a Dutch diminutive of **Anna**.

Annette *fem* a French diminutive of **Ann**, used as an English-language form.

Annika *fem* a Swedish diminutive of **Anna**.

Annis, Annice *fem* a medieval diminutive of **Agnes**.

Annona *fem* a variant form of **Anona**.

Annunciata *fem* Italian form of *nuntius*, bringer of news, i.e. the angel Gabriel, who delivered the announcement of the Virgin Mary's conception, a name often given to children born on 25 March, Lady Day (*Latin*).

Anona *fem* annual crops, hence the Roman goddess of crops (*Latin*); a variant form is **Annona**; diminutives are **Nonnie, Nona**.

Anora *fem* light, graceful (*Old English*).

Anscom *masc* one who dwells in a secret valley; a solitary person (*Old English*).

Anselm, Ansel *masc* a surname, meaning, god helmet, i.e. under the protection of God, used as a first name (*Germanic*).

Anselma *fem* form of **Anselm**; a variant form is **Arselma**.

Ansley *masc* a surname, meaning clearing with a hermitage or solitary dwelling, used as a first name (*Old English*).

Anson *masc* a surname, meaning son of Agnes or Anne,
    used as a first name (*Old English*).

Anstice *masc* a surname, meaning resurrected, used as
    a first name (*Greek*).

Anthea *fem* flowery (*Greek*).

Anthony *masc* a variant form of **Antony**; a diminutive
    form is **Tony**.

Antoine *masc* the French form of **Anthony**, now used
    independently as an English-language form; a variant
    form is **Antwan**.

Antoinette *fem* diminutive of **Antonia**, now used as an
    English-language form; a diminutive form is
    Toinette.

Anton *masc* a German form of **Antony**, now used as an
    English-language form.

Antonia *fem* form of **Antony**; diminutive forms are
    Toni, Tonia, Tonie, Tony.

Antonio *masc* the Italian and Spanish form of **Antony**.

Antony *masc* priceless; praiseworthy (*Latin*); a variant
    form is **Anthony**; a diminutive form is **Tony**.

Antwan *masc* a variant form of **Antoine**.

Anwell *masc* beloved (*Gaelic*).

Anwen *fem* very beautiful (*Welsh*).

Anyon *masc* anvil (*Gaelic*).

Aoife *fem* the Irish Gaelic form of **Eve**; a variant form
    is **Aefa**.

Aonghas *masc* Scots Gaelic form of **Angus**.

Aphra *fem* dust (*Hebrew*); woman from Carthage
(*Latin*).—a variant form is **Afra**.

April *fem* the name of the month, *Aprilis*, used as a
personal name (*Latin*).

Ara *fem* spirit of revenge, and the goddess of destruc-
tion and vengeance (*Greek*).

Arabella, Arabela *fem* a fair altar (*Latin*); a woman
(*Arabic*); diminutive forms are **Bella, Belle**.

Araminta *fem* beautiful, sweet-smelling flower
(*Greek*); a diminutive form is **Minta**.

Archard *masc* sacred and powerful (*Germanic*).

Archer *masc* a surname, meaning professional or
skilled bowman, used as a first name (*Old English*).

Archibald *masc* very bold; holy prince (*Germanic*);
diminutive forms are **Archie, Archy**.

Ardath *fem* field of flowers (*Hebrew*); variant forms
are **Aridatha, Ardatha**.

Ardal *masc* high valour (*Irish Gaelic*).

Ardella, Ardelle, Ardelis *fem* enthusiasm, warmth
(*Hebrew*).

Arden *masc* a surname, meaning dwelling place or
gravel or eagle valley, used as a surname (*Old
English*); burning, fiery (*Latin*).

Ardley *masc* from the domestic meadow (*Old English*).

Ardolph *masc* home-loving wolf rover (*Old English*).

Areta, Aretha *fem* excellently virtuous (*Greek*); variant
forms are **Aretta, Arette, Aretas**.

Argenta, Argente, Argente *fem* silver or silvery coloured (*Latin*).

Aretta, Arette *fem* variant forms of **Areta**.

Argus *masc* all-seeing, watchful one, from Argus Panoptes, a character from Greek mythology with a hundred eyes all over his body (*Greek*).

Argyle, Argyll *masc* the Scottish placename, meaning land or district of the Gaels, used as a first name (*Scots Gaelic*).

Aria *fem* the Italian word for beautiful melody, from *aer*, 'breeze' (*Latin*), used as a first name.

Ariadne *fem* very holy (*Greek*).

Arianna *fem* an Italian form of **Ariadne**.

Arianne *fem* a French form of **Ariadne**.

Aric *masc* sacred ruler (*Old English*); diminutive forms are **Rick, Rickie, Ricky**.

Ariel *masc* God's lion (*Hebrew*).

Ariella, Arielle *fem* forms of Ariel (*Hebrew*).

Aries *masc* the ram, the sign of the Zodiac for 21 March to 19 April (*Latin*).

Arlen *masc* pledge (*Irish Gaelic*).

Arlene *fem* form of **Arlen**; a variant form of **Charlene, Marlene**; variant forms are **Arleen, Arlena, Arlina, Arline, Arlyne**.

Arlie, Arley, Arly *masc* a surname, meaning eagle wood, used as a first name (*Old English*).

Armand *masc* a French form of **Herman**.

Armel *masc* stone prince or chief (*Breton Gaelic*).

Armelle *fem* form of Armel.

Armilla *fem* bracelet (*Latin*).

Armin *masc* military man (*Germanic*).

Armina, Armine *fem* forms of **Armin**; variant forms are **Erminie, Erminia**.

Armstrong *masc* a surname, meaning strong in the arm, used as a first name (*Old English*).

Arn *masc* diminutive of **Arnold, Arnulf**; a contraction of **Aaron**.

Arnalda *fem* form of **Arnold** (*Germanic*).

Arnall *masc* a surname variant form of **Arnold** used as a first name (*Germanic*).

Arnaud, Arnaut *masc* French forms of **Arnold**.

Arnatt, Arnett *masc* surname variant forms of **Arnold** used as first names.

Arne *masc* eagle (*Old Norse*); a diminutive form is **Arnie**.

Arno *masc* a diminutive of **Arnold, Arnulf**.

Arnold *masc* strong as an eagle (*Germanic*); eagle meadow (*Old English*); diminutive forms are **Arn, Arnie, Arno, Arny**.

Arnott *masc* a surname variant form of **Arnold** used as a first name.

Arnulf *masc* eagle wolf (*Germanic*); diminutives are **Arn, Arno**.

Arphad *masc* a variant form of **Arvad**.

Arselma *fem* a variant form of **Anselma**.

Artemas *masc* form of **Artemis** (*Greek*).

Artemis *fem* the name of the virgin Greek goddess of hunting and the moon, the derivation of which is unknown. The Roman equivalent is Diana.

Arthur *masc* eagle Thor (*Celtic*); a diminutive form is **Art**.

Arturo *masc* the Italian and Spanish forms of **Arthur**.

Arundel *masc* the English placename, meaning a valley where nettles grow, used as a first name (*Old English*).

Arva *fem* ploughed land, pasture (*Latin*).

Arvad *masc* wanderer (*Hebrew*); a variant form is **Arpad**.

Arval, Arvel *masc* greatly lamented (*Latin*).

Arvid *masc* eagle wood (*Norse*).

Arvin *masc* people's friend (*Germanic*).

Arwel *masc* meaning uncertain (*Welsh*).

Arwenna *fem* form of **Arwyn**.

Arwyn *masc* muse (*Welsh*); a variant form is **Awen**.

Asa *masc* healer, physician (*Hebrew*).

Asahel *masc* made of God (*Hebrew*).

Asaph *masc* a collector (*Hebrew*).

Ascot, Ascott *masc* an English placename and surname, meaning eastern cottages, used as a first name (*Old English*).

Ashburn *masc* a surname, meaning stream where the ash trees grow, used as a first name (*Old English*).

Ashby *masc* an English placename, meaning ash-tree

farmstead, used as a first name (*Old English*).

Asher *masc* happy, fortunate (*Hebrew*).

Ashford *masc* an English placename, meaning ford by a clump of ash trees, used as a first name (*Old English*).

Ashley, Ashleigh *masc*, *fem* the surname, meaning ash wood or glade, used as a first name (*Old English*).

Ashlin *masc* ash-surrounded pool (*Old English*).

Ashton *masc* an English placename, meaning ash-tree farmstead, used as a first name (*Old English*).

Ashur *masc* martial, warlike (*Semitic*).

Asphodel *fem* a daffodil-like plant, the origin of whose name is obscure, used as a first name (*Greek*).

Astra *fem* diminutive of **Astrid**.

Astrid *fem* fair god (*Norse*); a diminutive is **Astra**.

Atalanta, Atalante *fem* the name of a mythological character who agreed to marry the man who could outrun her (*Greek*); a variant form is **Atlanta**.

Atalya *fem* guardian (*Spanish*).

Athanasius *masc* immortal (*Greek*).

Athena, Ahthene, Athenée *fem* in Greek mythology, the goddess of wisdom. Her Roman counterpart is Minerva (*Greek*).

Atherton *masc* a surname, meaning noble army's place, used as a first name (*Old English*).

Athol, Atholl *masc* a placename and surname, meaning new Ireland, used as a first name (*Scots Gaelic*).

Atlante *fem* a variant form of **Atalanta**.

Atlee, Atley, Atley *masc* a surname, meaning at the
    wood or clearing, used as a first name (*Old English*).

Atwater, Atwatter *masc* a surname, meaning by the
    water, used as a first name (*Old English*).

Atwell *masc* a surname, meaning at the spring or well
    of, used as a first name (*Old English*).

Auberon *masc* noble bear (*Germanic*); a variant form is
    Oberon; a diminutive form is **Bron**.

Aubin *masc* a surname, meaning blond one, used as a
    first name (*French*).

Aubrey *masc* ruler of spirits (*Germanic*).

Audrey *fem* noble might (*Old English*).

August *masc* the Polish and German form of **Augustus**;
    the eighth month of the year, named after the Roman
    emperor **Augustus**, used as a first name.

Augusta *fem* form of **Augustus**; diminutive forms are
    Gussie, Gusta.

Auguste *masc* the French form of **Augustus**.

Augustin *masc* the German and French forms of
    Augustine.

Augustine *masc* belonging to **Augustus** (*Latin*); a
    diminutive form is **Gus**.

Augustus *masc* exalted; imperial (*Latin*); a diminutive
    form is **Gus**.

Aura, Aure, Aurea *fem* breath of air (*Latin*); a variant
    form is **Auria**.

Aurelia *fem* form of **Aurelius**.

Aurelius *masc* golden (*Latin*).

Auria *fem* a variant form of **Aura**.

Aurora *fem* morning redness; fresh; brilliant (*Latin*).

Austin *masc* a contraction of **Augustine**.

Autumn *fem* the name of the season, the origin of which is uncertain, used as a first name.

Ava *fem* origin uncertain, perhaps a Germanic diminutive of names beginning *Av*.

Avera *fem* transgressor (*Hebrew*); a variant form is **Aberah**.

Averil, Averill *fem* English forms of **Avril**.

Avery *masc* a surname, derived from **Alfred**, used as a surname (*Old English*).

Avice, Avis *fem* possibly bird (*Latin*).

Avril *fem* the French form of **April**.

Awen *masc* a variant form of **Arwyn**.

Axel *masc* father of peace (*Germanic*).

Aylmer *masc* a surname, meaning noble and famous, used as a first name (*Old English*).

Aylward *masc* a surname, meaning noble guardian, used as a first name (*Old English*).

Azaliea, Azalia, Azalee *fem* variant forms of the name of the azalea plant, supposed to prefer dry earth, used as a first name.

Azaria *fem* form of **Azarias**.

Azarias *masc* helped by God (*Hebrew*).

Azura, Azure *fem* blue as the sky (*French*).

B

Bab, Babs *fem* diminutive forms of **Barbara**.

Bailey, Baillie *masc* a surname, meaning bailiff or steward, used as a first name (*Old French*); a variant form is **Bayley**.

Bainbridge *masc* a surname, meaning bridge over a short river, used as a surname (*Old English*).

Baird *masc* a Scottish surname, meaning minstrel or bard, used as a first name (*Celtic*); a variant form is **Bard**.

Baldemar *masc* bold and famous prince (*Germanic*).

Baldovin *masc* the Italian form of **Baldwin**.

Baldric, Baldrick *masc* a surname, meaning princely or bold ruler, used as a first name (*Germanic*); a variant form is **Baudric**.

Baldwin *masc* bold friend (*Germanic*).

Balfour *masc* a surname from a Scottish placename, meaning village with pasture, used as a first name (*Scots Gaelic*).

Ballard *masc* a surname, meaning bald, used as a first name (*Old English, Old French*).

Balthasar, Balthazar *masc* Baal defend the king
(*Babylonian*).

Bambi *fem* a variant form of the word for *bambino*,
child (*Italian*).

Bancroft *masc* a surname, meaning bean place, used as
a first name (*Old English*).

Baptist *masc* a baptiser, purifier (*Greek*).

Baptista *fem* form of **Baptist**.

Baptiste *masc* a French form of **Baptist**.

Barbara, Barbra *fem* foreign, strange (*Greek*); diminutive forms are **Bab, Babs, Barbie**.

Barclay *masc* a surname, meaning birch wood, used as
a first name (*Old English*); variant forms are
Berkeley, Berkley.

Bard *masc* a variant form of **Baird**; a diminutive form
of **Bardolph**.

Bardolph *masc* bright wolf (*Germanic*).

Barlow *masc* a surname, meaning barley hill or barley
clearing, used as a first name (*Old English*).

Barnaby, Barnabas *masc* son of consolation and
exhortation (*Hebrew*); a diminutive form is **Barney**.

Barnard *masc* a variant form of **Bernard**; a diminutive
form is **Barney**.

Barnet, Barnett *masc* a surname, meaning land cleared
by burning, used as a first name (*Old English*).

Barnum *masc* a surname, meaning homestead of a
warrior, used as a first name (*Old English*).

Baron *masc* the lowest rank of the peerage used as a
   first name (*Old French*); a variant form is **Barron**.

Barratt, Barrett *masc* a surname, meaning commerce
   or trouble or strife, used as a first name (*Old French*).

Barron *masc* a variant form of **Baron**.

Barry *masc* spear (*Irish Gaelic*).

Bart *masc* a diminutive form of **Bartholomew,
   Bartley, Barton, Bartram**.

Barthold *masc* variant form of **Berthold**.

Bartholomew *masc* a warlike son (*Hebrew*); diminutive forms are **Bart, Bat**.

Bartley *masc* a surname, meaning a birch wood or
   clearing, used as a first name (*Old English*); a
   diminutive form is **Bart**.

Barton *masc* the surname, meaning farm or farmyard,
   used as a first name (*Old English*); a diminutive form
   is **Bart**.

Bartram *masc* a variant form of **Bertram**.

Barzillai *masc* man of iron (*Hebrew*).

Basil *masc* kingly; royal (*Greek*).

Basile *masc* the French form of **Basil**.

Basilia *fem* form of **Basil**.

Basilio *masc* the Italian and Spanish form of **Basil**.

Bat *masc* a diminutive form of **Bartholomew**.

Bathilda *fem* battle commander (*Germanic*).

Bathilde *fem* the French form of **Bathilda**.

Bathsheba *fem* daughter of plenty (*Hebrew*).

Batiste *masc* the French form of **Baptist**.

Battista *masc* the Italian form of **Baptist**.

Baudouin *masc* the French form of **Baldwin**.

Baudric *masc* a variant form of **Baldric**.

Bautista *masc* the Spanish form of **Baptist**.

Baxter *masc* a surname, meaning baker, used as a first name (*Old English*).

Bayley *masc* a variant form of **Bailey**.

Bea *fem* a diminutive form of **Beatrice, Beatrix**.

Beal, Beale, Beall *masc* a surname variant form of **Beau** used as a first name (*French*).

Beaman *masc* bee keeper (*Old English*); a variant form of **Beaumont** (*French*).

Beata *fem* blessed, divine one (*Latin*); a diminutive form is **Bea**.

Beatrice, Beatrix *fem* woman who blesses (*Latin*); diminutive forms are **Bea, Beatie, Beaty, Bee, Trix, Trixie**.

Beau *masc* handsome (*French*); a diminutive form of **Beaufort, Beamont**.

Beaufort *masc* a surname, meaning beautiful stronghold, used as a first name (*French*); a diminutive form is **Beau**.

Beaumont *masc* a surname, meaning beautiful hill, used as a first name (*French*); a diminutive form is **Beau**.

Beavan, Beaven *masc* variant forms of **Bevan**.

Beckie, Becky *fem* diminutive forms of **Rebecca**.

Beda *fem* maid of war (*Old English*).

Bee *fem* a diminutive form of **Beatrice**.

Belinda *fem* a name used by Sir John Vanburgh in his
    play *The Provok'd Wife*, its origin is uncertain,
    possibly beautiful woman (*Italian*).

Bella, Belle *fem* beautiful (*French, Italian*); diminutive
    forms of **Annabel, Arabella, Isabella**.

Bellamy *masc* a surname, meaning handsome friend,
    used as a first name (*Old French*).

Ben *masc* a diminutive form of **Benedict, Benjamin**,
    also used independently.

Bena *fem* wise one (*Hebrew*).

Benedetto *masc* the Italian form of **Benedict**.

Benedict, Benedick *masc* blessed (*Latin*); *also* **Bennet**;
    diminutives are **Ben, Bennie, Benny**.

Benedicta *fem* form of **Benedict**; a contracted form is
    Benita; a diminutive form is **Dixie**.

Benedikt *masc* the German form of **Benedict**.

Beniamino *masc* the Italian form of **Benjamin**.

Benita *fem* form of **Benito**; a contracted form of
    Benedicta.

Benito *masc* a Spanish form of **Benedict**.

Benjamin *masc* son of the right hand (*Hebrew*);
    diminutive forms are **Ben, Benjie, Bennie, Benny**.

Benjie *masc* a diminutive form of **Benjamin**.

Bennet *masc* a variant form of **Benedict**.

Bennie, Benny *masc* a diminutive form of **Benedict, Benjamin**.

Benoît *masc* the French form of **Benedict**.

Benson *masc* a surname, meaning son of **Ben**, used as a first name.

Bentley *masc* a surname from a Yorkshire placename, meaning woodland clearing where bent-grass grows, used as a first name(*Old English*).

Beppe, Beppo *masc* a diminutive form of **Giuseppe**, occasionally used independently.

Berenice *fem* bringing victory (*Greek*); *also* **Bernice**.

Berkeley, Berkley *masc* variant forms of **Barclay**.

Bernadette *fem* form of **Bernard**.

Bernard *masc* strong or hardy bear (*Germanic*); *also* **Barnard**; diminutive forms are **Barney, Bernie**.

Bernardin *masc* a French form of **Bernard**.

Bernardino *masc* an Italian diminutive form of **Bernard**.

Bernardo *masc* a Spanish and Italian form of **Bernard**.

Bernhard, Bernhardt *masc* a German form of **Bernard**.

Bernice *fem* a variant form of **Berenice**.

Bernie *masc* a diminutive form of **Bernard**.

Bert *masc* diminutive forms of **Albert, Bertram, Egbert, Gilbert**, etc..

Berta *fem* a German, Italian and Spanish form of **Bertha**.

Bertha *fem* bright; beautiful; famous (*Germanic*); a
diminutive form is **Bertie**.

Berthe *fem* the French form of **Bertha**.

Berthilda, Berthilde, Bertilda, Bertilde *fem* shining
maid of war (*Old English*).

Berthold *masc* bright ruler (*Germanic*); variant forms
are **Barthold, Bertold, Berthoud**; diminutive forms
are **Bert, Bertie**.

Bertie *masc* diminutive forms of **Albert, Bertram,
Egbert, Gilbert, Herbert**, etc; *fem* a diminutive form
of **Bertha**.

Bertold, Berthoud *masc* variant forms of **Berthold**.

Bertram *masc* bright; fair; illustrious (*Germanic*); a
variant form is **Bartram**; diminutive forms are **Bert,
Bertie**.

Bertrand *masc* the French form of **Bertram**.

Beryl *fem* jewel (*Greek*), the name of the gemstone
used as a first name.

Bess, Bessie *fem* diminutive forms of **Elizabeth**.

Beth *fem* a diminutive form of **Elizabeth, Bethany**,
now used independently.

Bethan *fem* a Welsh diminutive form of **Elizabeth-Ann**
also used independently.

Bethany *fem* a placename near Jerusalem, the home of
Lazarus in the New Testament and meaning house of
poverty, used as a first name (*Aramaic*).

Betsy, Bette, Bettina, Betty *fem* diminutive forms of

Elizabeth.

Beulah *fem* married (*Hebrew*).

Bevan *masc* a surname, meaning son of **Evan**, used as
a first name (*Welsh*); variant forms are **Beavan**,
Beaven, Bevin.

Beverley, Beverly *fem masc* a placename, meaning
beaver stream, used as a first name (*Old English*); a
diminutive form is **Bev**.

Bevin *masc* a surname, meaning drink wine, used as a
first name; a variant form of Bevan.

Bevis *masc* bull (*French*).

Bianca *fem* the Italian form of **Blanch**, now also used
independently as an English-language form.

Biddy *fem* a diminutive form of **Bridget.**

Bije *masc* a diminutive form of **Abijah**.

Bill *masc* a diminutive form of **William**.

Billie *masc* a diminutive form of **William**; *fem* a
diminutive form of **Wilhelmina**.

Bina, Binah, Bine *fem* bee (*Hebrew*).

Bing *masc* a surname, meaning a hollow, used as a first
name (*Germanic*).

Binnie *fem* a diminutive form of **Sabina**.

Birch *masc* a surname, from the birch tree, used as a
first name (*Old English*); a variant form is **Birk**.

Birgit *fem* the Swedish form of **Bridget**; a diminutive
form is **Britt**.

Birk *masc* a variant form of **Birch**.

Bishop *masc* a surname, meaning one who worked in a
   bishop's household, used as a first name (*Old English*).

Björn *masc* bear (*Old Norse*).

Black *masc* a surname, meaning dark-complexioned or
   dark-haired, used as a first name (*Old English*); a
   variant form is **Blake**.

Blair *masc* a placename and surname, meaning a plain,
   used as a first name (*Scottish Gaelic*).

Blaise *masc* sprouting forth (*French*).

Blake *masc* a variant form of Black; alternatively, pale
   or fair-complexioned (*Old English*).

Blanca *fem* the Spanish form of **Blanch**.

Blanche *fem* white (*Germanic*).

Bleddyn *masc* wolf (*Welsh*).

Bliss *masc, fem* a surname, meaning happiness or joy,
   used as a first name (*Old English*).

Blodwen *fem* white flower (*Welsh*).

Blossom *fem* like a flower (*Old English*).

Blyth, Blythe *masc, fem* a surname, meaning cheerful
   and gentle, used as a first name (*Old English*).

Boas, Boaz *masc* fleetness (Hebrew).

Bob, Bobbie, Bobby *masc* diminutive forms of
   Robert.

Bonar *masc* a surname, meaning gentle, kind, courteous, used as a first name (*French*); variant forms are
   Bonnar, Bonner.

Boniface *masc* doer of good (*Latin*).

Bonita *fem* pretty (*Spanish*); good (*Latin*); a diminutive form is **Bonnie**.

Bonnar, Bonner *masc* variant forms of **Bonar**.

Bonnie *fem* pretty (*Scots English*); a diminutive form of **Bonita**.

Booth *masc* a surname, meaning hut or shed, used as a first name (*Old Norse*).

Boris *masc* small (*Russian*).

Botolf, Botolph *masc* herald wolf (*Old English*).

Bourn, Bourne *masc* variant forms of **Burn**.

Bowen *masc* a surname, meaning son of Owen, used as a first name (*Welsh*).

Bowie *masc* a surname, meaning yellow-haired, used as a first name (*Scots Gaelic*).

Boyce *masc* a surname, meaning a wood, used as a first name (*Old French*).

Boyd *masc* a surname, meaning light-haired, used as a first name (*Scots Gaelic*).

Boyne *masc* the name of an Irish river, meaning white cow, used as a first name (*Irish Gaelic*).

Brad *masc* a diminutive form of **Bradley**, now used independently.

Bradford *masc* a placename and surname, meaning place at the broad ford, used as a first name (*Old English*).

Bradley *masc* a surname, meaning broad clearing or

broad wood, used as a first name (*Old English*); a diminutive form is **Brad**.

Brady *masc* a surname, of unknown meaning, used as a first name (*Irish Gaelic*).

Braham *masc* a surname, meaning house or meadow with broom bushes, used as a first name.

Bram *masc* a diminutive form of **Abram, Abraham**.

Bramwell *masc* a surname, meaning from the bramble spring, used as a first name (*Old English*).

Bran *masc* raven (*Gaelic*).

Brand *masc* firebrand (*Old English*).

Brandon *masc* a surname, meaning broom-covered hill, used as a first name (*Old English*); a variant form of **Brendan**.

Branwen *fem* raven-haired beauty (*Welsh*); a variant form of **Bronwen**.

Brenda *fem* a brand or sword (*Old Norse*).

Brendan *masc* prince (*Celtic*); a variant form is **Brandon**.

Brenna *fem* raven-haired beauty (*Irish Gaelic*).

Brent *masc* a surname, meaning a steep place, used as a first name (*Old English*).

Bret, Brett *masc* a Breton (*Old French*).

Brewster *masc* a surname, meaning brewer, used as a first name (*Old English*).

Brian *masc* strong (*Celtic*); a variant form is **Bryan**.

Brice *masc* a surname, of unknown meaning, used as a

first name (*Celtic*); a variant form is **Bryce**.

Bridget *fem* goddess of fire (*Celtic*); a variant form is **Brigid**; diminutive forms are **Biddy, Bridie**.

Brigham *masc* a surname, meaning homestead by a bridge, used as a first name (*Old English*).

Brigid *fem* a variant form of **Bridget**.

Brigide *fem* a Spanish, Italian, and French form of **Brid-get**.

Brigitte *fem* a French form of **Bridget**.

Briony *fem* a variant form of **Bryony**.

Britt *fem* a diminutive form of **Birgit**, now used independently.

Brittany *fem* the anglicized name of a French region, meaning land of the figured, or tattooed folk, used as a first name.

Brock *masc* a surname, meaning badger, used as a first name (*Old English*).

Broderic, Broderick *masc* a surname, meaning son of Roderick, used as a first name (*Welsh*); brother (*Scots Gaelic*).

Brodie, Brody *masc* a surname, meaning ditch, used as a first name (*Scots Gaelic*).

Bron *masc* a diminutive form of **Auberon, Oberon**.

Bronwen *fem* white breast (*Welsh*); variant forms are **Bronwyn, Branwen**.

Brook, Brooke *masc, fem* a surname, meaning stream, used as a first name; a variant form is **Brooks**.

Brooks *masc* a variant form of Brook.

Bruce *masc* a surname, meaning unknown, used as a first name (*Old French*).

Brunella fem form of Bruno.

Brunhilda, Brunhilde *fem* warrior maid (*Germanic*).

Bruno *masc* brown (*Germanic*).

Bryan *masc* a variant form of **Brian**.

Bryce *masc* a variant form of **Brice**.

Bryn *masc* hill (*Welsh*).

Brynmor *fem* large hill (*Welsh*).

Bryony *fem* the name of a climbing plant used as a first name (*Greek*); a variant form is **Briony**.

Buck *masc* stag; he-goat; a lively young man (*Old English*).

Buckley *masc* a surname, meaning stag or he-goat meadow, used as a first name (*Old English*).

Budd, Buddy *masc* the informal term for a friend or brother used as a first name (*Old English*).

Buena *fem* good (*Spanish*).

Bunty *fem* a diminutive meaning lamb, now used as a first name (*English*).

Buona *fem* good (*Italian*).

Burchard *masc* a variant form of **Burkhard**.

Burdon *masc* a surname, meaning castle on a hill or valley with a cowshed, used as a first name (*Old English*).

Burford *masc* a surname, meaning ford by a castle,

used as a first name (*Old English*).

Burgess *masc* a surname, meaning citizen or inhabitant of a borough, used as a first name (*Old French*).

Burk, Burke *masc* a surname, meaning fort or manor, used as a first name (*Old French*).

Burkhard *masc* strong as a castle (*Germanic*); a variant form is **Burchard**.

Burl *masc* cup bearer (*Old English*).

Burley *masc* dweller in the castle by the meadow (*Old English*); a diminutive form is **Burleigh**.

Burn, Burne *masc* a surname, meaning brook or stream, used as a first name (*Old English*); variant forms are **Bourn, Bourne, Byrne**.

Burnett *masc* a surname, meaning brown-complexioned or brown-haired, used as a first name (*Old French*).

Burt *masc* a diminutive form of **Burton**, now used independently.

Burton *masc* a surname, meaning farmstead of a fortified placed, used as a first name (*Old English*); diminutive forms are **Burt**.

Buster *masc* an informal term of address for a boy or young man, now used as a first name (*English*).

Byrne *masc* a variant form of **Burn**.

Byron *masc* a surname, meaning at the cowsheds, used as a first name (*Old English*).

C

Caddie *fem* a diminutive form of **Carol, Carola, Carole, Caroline, Carolyn**.

Caddick, Caddock *masc* a surname, meaning decrepit or epileptic, used as a first name (*Old French*).

Cadell *masc* a surname, meaning battle spirit, used as a first name (*Welsh*).

Cadence *fem* rhythmic (*Latin*).

Cadenza *fem* the Italian form of **Cadence**.

Cadmus *masc* man from the east; in Greek mythology a Phoenician prince who founded Thebes with five warriors he had created (*Greek*).

Cadwallader *masc* battle arranger (*Welsh*).

Caesar *masc* long-haired; the Roman title of emperor used as a first name (*Latin*).

Cain *masc* possession; the Biblical character who killed his brother Abel (*Hebrew*).

Cáit *fem* the Irish Gaelic form of Kate.

Caitlín, Caitrín *fem* Irish Gaelic forms of **Katherine**.

Cal *fem* a diminutive form of **Calandra, Calantha**.

Calandra *fem* lark(*Greek*); diminutive forms are **Cal,**

Callie, Cally.

Calandre *fem* the French form of **Calandra**.

Calandria *fem* the Spanish form of **Calandra**.

Calantha *fem* beautiful blossom (*Greek*); diminutive forms are **Cal, Callie, Cally**.

Calanthe *fem* the French form of **Calantha**.

Calder *masc* a placename and surname, meaning hard or rapid water, used as a first name (*Celtic*).

Caldwell *masc* a surname, meaning cold spring or stream, used as a first name (*Old English*).

Caleb *masc* a dog (*Hebrew*); a diminutive form is **Cale**.

Caledonia *fem* the Roman name for Scotland used as a first name (*Latin*).

Caley *masc* thin, slender (*Irish Gaelic*); diminutive form of **Calum**.

Calhoun *masc* a surname, meaning from the forest, used as a first name (*Irish Gaelic*).

Calla *fem* beautiful (*Greek*).

Callie *fem* a diminutive form of **Calandra, Calantha**.

Calliope *fem* lovely voice; the muse of poetry (*Greek*).

Callisto *masc* most fair or good (*Greek*).

Callista *fem* form of **Callisto**.

Cally *fem* a diminutive form of **Calandra, Calantha**; *masc* diminutive form of **Calum**.

Calum, Callum *masc* the Scots Gaelic form of *Columba*, the Latin for dove; a diminutive form of **Malcolm**; diminutive forms are **Cally, Caley**.

Calumina *fem* form of **Calum**.

Calvert *masc* a surname, meaning calf herd, used as a
    first name (*Old English*).

Calvin *masc* little bald one (*Latin*).

Calvina *fem* form of **Calvin**.

Calvino *masc* and Italian and Spanish forms of **Calvin**.

Calypso *fem* concealer; in Greek mythology, the sea
    nymph who held Odysseus captive for seven years
    (*Greek*).a variant form is **Kalypso**.

Cameron *masc* a surname, meaning hook nose, used as
    a first name (*Scots Gaelic*).

Camila *fem* the Spanish form of **Camilla**.

Camilla *fem* votaress, attendant at a sacrifice (*Latin*).

Camille *masc*, *fem* the French form of **Camilla**.

Campbell *masc* a surname, meaning crooked mouth,
    used as a first name (*Scots Gaelic*).

Candie *fem* a diminutive form of **Candice, Candida**.

Candice, Candace *fem* meaning uncertain, possibly
    brilliantly white or pure and virtuous, the name of an
    Ethiopian queen (*Latin*); **Candie, Candy**.

Candida *fem* shining white (*Latin*); diminutive forms
    are **Candie, Candy**.

Candy *fem* a diminutive form of **Candice, Candida**; a
    name used in its own right, from candy, the American
    English word for a sweet.

Canice *masc* handsome or fair one (*Irish Gaelic*).

Canute *masc* knot (*Old Norse*), the name of a Danish

king of England (1016–35); variant forms are **Cnut**,
Knut.

Cara *fem* friend (*Irish Gaelic*); dear, darling (*Italian*); a
variant form is **Carina**.

Caradoc, Caradog *masc* beloved (*Welsh*); a variant
form is **Cradoc**.

Cardew *masc* a surname meaning black fort, used as a
first name (*Welsh*).

Carey *masc* a surname, meaning castle dweller (*Welsh*)
or son of the dark one (*Irish Gaelic*), used as a first
name; a variant form of **Cary**.

Caridad *fem* the Spanish form of **Charity**.

Carina *fem* a variant form of **Cara**.

Carissa *fem* dear one (*Latin*).

Carl *masc* an anglicized German and Swedish form of
Charles; a diminutive form of **Carlton, Carlin,
Carlisle, Carlo, Carlos**.

Carla *fem* form of **Carl**; a variant form is **Carlin**;
diminutive forms are **Carlie, Carley, Carly**.

Carleton *masc* a variant form of **Carlton**.

Carlie *fem* a diminutive form of **Carla, Carlin**.

Carlin *fem* a variant form of **Carla**; diminutive forms
are **Carlie, Carley, Carly**.

Carlo *masc* the Italian form of **Charles**.

Carlos *masc* the Spanish form of **Charles**.

Carlotta *fem* the Italian form of **Charlotte**.

Carlton *masc* a placename and surname, meaning farm

of the churls—a rank of peasant, used as a first name
(*Old English*).variant forms are **Carleton, Charlton,
Charleston**; a diminutive form is **Carl**.

Carly *fem* a diminutive form of **Carla, Carlin**, now
used independently.

Carmel *fem* garden (*Hebrew*).

Carmela *fem* a Spanish and the Italian forms of
Carmel.

Carmelita *fem* a Spanish diminutive form of **Carmel**.

Carmen *fem* a Spanish form of **Carmel**.

Carmichael *masc* a Scottish placename and surname,
meaning fort of **Michael**, used as a first name (*Celtic*).

Carnation *fem* the name of a flour, meaning flesh
colour, used as a first name (*Latin/French*).

Carol *masc* a shortened form of *Carolus*, the Latin
form of **Charles**; *fem* a shortened form of **Caroline**;
diminutive forms are **Caro, Carrie, Caddie**.

Carola *fem* a variant form of **Caroline**; diminutive
forms are **Carrie, Caro, Caddie**.

Carole *fem* the French form of **Carol**; a contracted
form of **Caroline**; diminutive forms are **Caro,
Carrie, Caddie**.

Carolina *fem* the Italian and Spanish forms of
Caroline.

Caroline, Carolyn *fem* form of *Carolus*, the Latin form
of **Charles**; diminutive forms are **Caro, Carrie,
Caddie**.

Carr *masc* a placename and surname, meaning over-
grown marshy ground, used as a first name (*Old
Norse*); variant forms are **Karr, Kerr**.

Carrie *fem* a diminutive form of **Carol, Carola,
Carole, Caroline, Carolyn**.

Carrick *masc* a placename, meaning rock, used as a
first name (*Gaelic*).

Carroll *masc* a surname, of uncertain meaning—
possibly hacking, used as a first name (*Irish Gaelic*).

Carson *masc* a surname, of uncertain meaning but
possibly marsh dweller (*Old English*), used as a first
name.

Carter *masc* a surname, meaning a driver or maker of
cars (*Old English*) or son of Arthur (*Scots Gaelic*),
used as a first name.

Carver *masc* great rock (*Cornish Gaelic*); a surname,
meaning sculptor, used as a first name (*Old English*).

Carwyn *masc* blessed love (*Welsh*).

Cary *masc* a surname, meaning pleasant stream, used
as a first name (*Celtic*); a variant form is **Carey**.

Carys *fem* love (Welsh).

Casey *masc fem* an Irish surname, meaning vigilant,
used as a first name; a placename, Cayce in Ken-
tucky, where the hero Casey Jones was born, used as
a first name; *fem* a variant form of **Cassie** used
independently.

Cashel *masc* a placename, meaning circular stone fort,

used as a first name (*Irish Gaelic*).

Casimir *masc* the English form of **Kasimir**.

Caspar, Casper *masc* the Dutch form of **Jasper**, now also used as an English-language form.

Cass *fem* a diminutive form of **Cassandra**; *masc* a diminutive form of **Cassidy, Cassius**.

Cassandra *fem* she who inflames with love (*Greek*); in Greek mythology, a princess whose prophecies of doom were not believed; diminutive forms are **Cass, Cassie**.

Cassidy *masc* a surname, meaning clever, used as a first name (*Irish Gaelic*); a diminutive form is **Cass**.

Cassie *fem* a diminutive form of **Cassandra**.

Cassian, Cassius *masc* a Roman family name, of uncertain meaning—possibly empty, used as a first name (*Latin*); a diminutive form is **Cass**.

Castor *masc* beaver (*Greek*).

Catalina *fem* the Spanish form of **Katherine**.

Caterina *fem* the Italian form of **Katherine**.

Cathal *masc* battle ruler (*Irish Gaelic*).

Catharina, Catharine, Catherina *fem* variant forms of **Catherine**.

Catherine *fem* the French form of **Katherine**, now used as an English-language form; diminutive forms are **Cath, Cathie, Cathy**.

Cato *masc* a Roman family name, meaning wise one, used as a first name (*Latin*).

Catrin *fem* the Welsh form of **Katherine**.

Catriona *fem* the Scots Gaelic form of **Katherine**.

Cavan *masc* a placename, meaning hollow with a grassy hill, used as a first name (*Irish Gaelic*); a variant form is **Kavan**.

Cecil *masc* dim-sighted (*Latin*).

Cecile *fem* the French form of **Cecily, Cecilia**.

Cécile *masc* the French form of **Cecil**.

Cecily, Cecilia *fem* forms of **Cecil**; diminutive forms are **Celia, Cis, Cissie, Cissy**; a variant form is **Cicely**.

Cedric *masc* a name adapted by Sir Walter Scott for a character in *Ivanhoe* from the Saxon *Cerdic*, the first king of Wessex.

Ceinwen beautiful and blessed (*Welsh*).

Celandine *fem* the name of either of two unrelated flowering plants, meaning swallow, used as a first name (*Greek*).

Celeste, Celestine *fem* heavenly (*Latin*).

Celia *fem* heavenly (*Latin*); dimin of **Cecilia**.

Cemlyn *masc* a placename, meaning bending lake, used as a first name.

Cendrillon *fem* from the ashes, the fairytale heroine (*French*); the anglicized form is **Cinderella**.

Cephas *masc* a stone (*Aramaic*).

Ceri *masc* love (*Welsh*).

Cerian *fem* diminutive form of **Ceri**.

Cerys *fem* love (*Welsh*).

César *masc* the French form of **Caesar**.

Cesare *masc* the Italian form of **Caesar**.

Chad *masc* meaning uncertain—possibly warlike, bellicose (*Old English*).

Chaim *masc* a variant form of **Hyam**.

Chance *masc* the abstract noun for the quality of good fortune used as a first name (*Old French*); a variant form of **Chauncey**.

Chancellor *masc* a surname, meaning counsellor or secretary, used as a first name (*Old French*).

Chancey *masc* a variant form of **Chauncey**.

Chandler *masc* a surname, meaning maker or seller of candles, used as a first name (*Old French*).

Chandra *fem* moon brighter than the stars (*Sanskrit*).

Chanel *fem* the surname of the French couturier and perfumier, Coco Chanel, used as a first name.

Chapman *masc* a surname, meaning merchant, used as a first name (*Old English*).

Charis *fem* grace (*Greek*).

Charity *fem* the abstract noun for the quality of tolerance or genorosity used as a personal name (*Old French*).

Charlene *fem* a relatively modern diminutive form of **Charles**.

Charles *masc* strong; manly; noble-spirited (*Germanic*); a diminutive form is **Charlie, Charley**.

Charlie, Charley *masc, fem* diminutive forms of **Charles, Charlotte**.

Charlotte *fem* form of **Charles** (*Germanic*); diminutive forms are **Charlie, Charley, Lottie**.

Charlton, Charleton *masc* variant forms of **Carlton**.

Charmaine *fem* a diminutive form of the abstract noun for the quality of pleasing or attracting people used as a first name; a variant form of **Charmian**.

Charmian *fem* little delight (*Greek*); a modern variant form is **Charmaine**.

Chase *masc* a surname, meaning hunter, used as a first name (*Old French*).

Chauncey, Chaunce *masc* a surname, of uncertain meaning—possibly chancellor, used as a first name (*Old French*); variant forms are **Chance, Chancey**.

Chelsea *fem* a placename, meaning chalk landing place, used as a first name (*Old English*).

Cher, Chérie *fem* dear, darling (*French*).

Cherry *fem* the name of the fruit used as a first name; a form of **Chérie**; a variant form is **Cheryl**.

Cheryl *fem* a variant form of **Cherry**; a combining form of **Cherry** and **Beryl**; a variant form is **Sheryl**.

Chester *masc* a placename, meaning Roman fortified camp, used as a first name (*Old English*).

Chiara *fem* the Italian form of **Clara**.

Chilton *masc* a placename and surname, meaning children's farm, used as a first name (*Old English*).

Chiquita *fem* little one (*Spanish*).

Chloë, Chloe *fem* a green herb; a young shoot (*Greek*).

Chloris *fem* green (*Greek*).

Chris *masc fem* a diminutive form of **Christian,
Christine, Christopher**.

Chrissie *fem* a diminutive form of **Christiana,
Christine**.

Christabel *fem* a combination of **Christine** and **Bella**
made by Samuel Taylor Coleridge for a poem of this
name.

Christian *masc, fem* belonging to Christ; a believer in
Christ (*Latin*); diminutive forms are **Chris, Christie,
Christy**.

Christiana *fem* form of Christian; a variant form is
Christina.

Christie *masc* a surname, meaning Christian, used as a
first name; a diminutive form of **Christian,
Christopher**; *fem* a diminutive form of **Christian,
Christine**; a variant form is **Christy**.

Christina *fem* a variant form of **Christiana**.

Christine *fem* a French form of **Christina**, now used as
an English-language form; diminutive forms are
Chris, Chrissie, Christie, Christy, Teenie, Tina.

Christmas *masc* festival of Christ (*Old English*).

Christoph *masc* the German form of **Christopher**.

Christopher *masc* bearing Christ (*Greek*); diminutive
forms are **Chris, Christie, Christy, Kester, Kit**.

Christy *masc fem* a variant form of **Christie**.

Chrystal *fem* a variant form of **Crystal**.

Churchill *masc* a placename and surname, meaning
church on a hill, used as a first name (*Old English*).

Cian *masc* ancient (*Irish Gaelic*); anglicized forms are
Kean, Keane.

Ciara *fem* form of **Ciarán**.

Ciarán *masc* small and black (*Irish Gaelic*); the
anglicized form is **Kieran**.

Cicely *fem* a variant form of **Cecilia**.

Cilla *fem* a diminutive form of **Priscilla** (*French*).

Cinderella *fem* the anglicized form of **Cendrillon**, the
fairytale heroine; diminutive forms are **Cindie,
Cindy, Ella**.

Cindy *fem* a diminuntive form of **Cinderella, Cynthia,
Lucinda**, now often used independently.

Cinzia *fem* the Italian form of **Cynthia**.

Claiborne *masc* a variant form of **Clayborne**; a
diminutive form is **Clay**.

Claire *fem* the French form of **Clara**, now used widely
as an English form.

Clara *fem* bright, illustrous (*Latin*); a variant form is
Clare; a diminutive form is **Clarrie**.

Clarabel, Clarabella, Clarabelle *fem* a combination of
Clara and **Bella** or **Belle**, meaning bright, shining
beauty (*Latin/French*); a variant form is **Claribel**.

Clare *fem* a variant form of **Clara**; *fem, masc* a surname, meaning or bright, shining, used as a first name
(*Latin*).

Clarence *masc* bright, shining (*Latin*); a diminutive
   form is **Clarrie**.

Claribel *fem* a variant form of **Clarabel**.

Clarice *fem* fame (*Latin*); a variant form of **Clara**; a
   variant form is **Clarissa**.

Clarinda *fem* a combination of **Clara** and **Belinda** or
   Lucinda.

Clarissa *fem* a variant form of **Clarice**.

Clark, Clarke *masc* a surname, meaning cleric, scholar
   or clerk, used as a first name (*Old French*).

Clarrie *fem* a diminutive form of **Clara**; *masc* a
   diminutive form of **Clarence**.

Claud *masc* the English form of **Claudius**.

Claude *masc* the French form of **Claud**; *fem* the French
   form of **Claudia**.

Claudia *fem* form of **Claud**.

Claudio *masc* the Italian and Spanish form of **Claud**.

Claudius *masc* lame (*Latin*); the Dutch and German
   forms of **Claud**.

Claus *masc* a variant form of **Klaus**.

Clay *masc* a surname, meaning a dweller in a place
   with clay soil, used as a first name (*Old English*); a
   diminutive form of **Claiborne, Clayborne, Clayton**.

Clayborne *masc* a surname, meaning a dweller in a
   place with clay soil by a brook, used as a first name
   (*Old English*); a variant form is Claiborne; a diminutive form is **Clay**.

Clayton *masc* a placename and surname, meaning place
in or with good clay, used as a first name (*Old
English*); a diminutive form is **Clay**.

Clem *fem* a diminutive form of **Clematis, Clemence,
Clemency, Clementine, Clementina**; *masc* a diminutive form of **Clement**.

Clematis *fem* climbing plant (*Greek*), the name of a
climbing plant with white, blue or purple flowers
used as a first name; diminutive forms are **Clem,
Clemmie**.

Clemency *fem* the abstract noun for the quality of
tempering justice with mercy used as a first name
(*Latin*); a variant form is **Clemence**; diminutive
forms are **Clem, Clemmie**.

Clement *masc* mild-tempered, merciful (*Latin*); a
diminutive form is **Clem**.

Clementine, Clementina *fem* forms of **Clement**;
diminutive forms are **Clem, Clemmie**.

Cleo *fem* a short form of **Cleopatra**, used independently.

Cleopatra *fem* father's glory (*Greek*); a diminutive
form is **Cleo**.

Cleveland *masc* a placename, meaning land of hills,
used as a first name (*Old English*).

Cliantha *fem* glory flower (*Greek*); a diminutive form
is **Clia**.

Cliff *masc* a diminutive form of **Clifford**, now used

independently.

Clifford *masc* a surname, meaning ford at a cliff, used as a first name (*Old English*); a diminutive form is **Cliff**.

Clifton *masc* a placename, meaning place on a cliff, used as a first name (*Old English*).

Clint *masc* a diminutive form of Clinton, now used independently.

Clinton *masc* a placename and surname, meaning settlement on a hill, used as a first name; a diminutive form is **Clint**.

Clio *fem* glory (*Greek*).

Clive *masc* a surname, meaning at the cliff, used as a first name (*Old English*).

Clorinda *fem* a combination of **Chloris** and **Belinda** or **Lucinda**.

Clothilde, Clotilde *fem* famous fighting woman (*Germanic*).

Clover *fem* the name of a flowering plant used as a first name (*English*).

Clovis *masc* warrior (*Germanic*).

Clyde *masc* the name of a Scottish river, meaning cleansing one, used as a first name.

Cnut *masc* a variant form of **Canute**.

Cody *masc* a surname used as a first name.

Colby *masc* From the dark country (*Norse*).

Col *masc* a diminutive form of **Colman, Columba**.

Cole *masc* a diminutive form of **Coleman, Colman, Nicholas**; a surname, meaning swarthy or coal-black, used as a first name (*Old English*).

Coleman *masc* a surname, meaning swarthy man or servant of Nicholas, used as a surname (*Old English*).

Colette *fem* a diminutive form of **Nicole**, now used independently; a variant form is **Collette**.

Colin *masc* a diminutive form of **Nicholas**, long used independently.

Colleen *fem* the Irish word for a girl used as a first name.

Collette *fem* a variant form of **Colette**.

Collier, Collyer *masc* a surname, meaning charcoal seller or buirner, used as a first name (*Old English*); a variant form is **Colyer**.

Colm *masc* dove (*Irish Gaelic/Latin*)

Colman, Colmán *masc* keeper of doves (*Irish Gaelic/Latin*); diminutive forms are **Col, Cole**.

Colombe *masc, fem* the French form of Columba.

Columba *masc, fem* dove (*Latin*); a diminutive form is **Coly**.

Columbine *fem* little dove; the name of a flowering plant used as a first name (*Latin*).

Colyer *masc* a variant form of **Collier**.

Comfort *fem* the abstract noun for the state of well-being or bringer of solace used as a first name, in the Puritan tradition (*Latin/French*).

Comyn *masc* bent (*Irish Gaelic*).

Con *masc* a diminutive form of **Conan, Connall, Connor, Conrad**; *fem* a diminutive form of **Constance**, etc.

Conan, Cónán *masc* little hound (*Irish Gaelic*); a diminutive form is **Con**.

Concepcion *fem* beginning, conception, a reference to the Immaculate Conception of the Virgin Mary (*Spanish*); diminutive forms are **Concha, Conchita**.

Concepta *fem* the Latin form of **Concetta**.

Concetta *fem* conceptive, a reference to the Virgin Mary and the Immaculate Conception (*Italian*).

Concha, Conchita *fem* diminutive forms of **Concepción**.

Conn *masc* chief (*Celtic*).

Connall *masc* courageous (*Irish and Scots Gaelic*).

Connor *masc* high desire or will (*Irish Gaelic*).

Conrad *masc* able counsellor (*Germanic*); a diminutive form is **Con**.

Conroy *masc* wise (*Gaelic*).

Consolata *fem* consoling, a reference to the Virgin Mary (*Italian*).

Consolation *fem* the abstract noun for the act of consoling or the state of solace used as a first name in the Puritan tradition.

Constance *fem* form of **Constant**; diminutive forms are **Con, Connie**; a variant form is **Constanta**.

Constant *masc* firm; faithful (*Latin*); a diminutive form is **Con**.

Constanta *fem* a variant form of **Constance**.

Constantine *masc* resolute; firm (*Latin*).

Constanza *fem* the Italian and Spanish forms of **Constance**.

Consuela *fem* consolation, a reference to the Virgin Mary (*Spanish*).

Consuelo *masc* consolation, a reference to the Virgin Mary (*Spanish*).

Conway *masc* a surname, of uncertain meaning—possibly yellow hound or head-smashing, used as a first name (*Irish Gaelic*); high or holy water (*Welsh*).

Cooper *masc* a surname, meaning barrel maker, used as a first name (*Old English*); a diminutive form is **Coop**.

Cora *fem* maiden (*Greek*).

Corabella, Corabelle *fem* beautiful maiden, a combination of **Cora** and **Bella**.

Coral *fem* the name of the pink marine jewel material used as a first name.

Coralie *fem* the French form of **Coral**.

Corazón *fem* (sacred) heart (Spanish).

Corbet, Corbett *masc* a surname, meaning raven, black-haired or raucousness, used as a first name (*Old French*).

Corcoran *masc* a surname, meaning red- or purple-faced, used as a first name (*Irish Gaelic*).

Cordelia *fem* warm-hearted (*Latin*).

Corey *masc* a surname, meaning god peace, used as a first name (*Irish Gaelic*).

Corinna, Corinne *fem* variant forms of **Cora**.

Cormac, Cormack, Cormick *masc* charioteer (*Irish Gaelic*).

Cornelia *fem* form of **Cornelius**.

Cornelius *masc* origin uncertain, possibly horn-like, a Roman family name; a variant form is **Cornell**.

Cornell masc a surname, meaning Cornwall or a hill where corn is sold, used as a first name; a variant form of **Cornelius**.

Corona *fem* crown (*Latin*).

Corrado *masc* the Italian form of **Conrad**.

Corwin *masc* friend of the heart (*Old French*)

Cosima *fem* form of **Cosmo**.

Cosimo *masc* an Italian form of **Cosmo**.

Cosmo *masc* order, beauty (*Greek*).

Costanza *fem* an Italian form of **Constance**.

Courtney *masc, fem* a surname, meaning short nose, used as a first name (*Old French*).

Cradoc *masc* a variant form of **Caradoc**.

Craig *masc* a surname meaning crag, used as a first name (*Scots Gaelic*).

Cranley *masc* a surname, meaning crane clearing, spring or meadow, used as a first name (*Old English*).

Crawford *masc* a placename and surname, meaning

ford of the crows, used as a first name (*Old English*).

Creighton *masc* a surname, meaning rock or cliff place (*Old Welsh*, *Old English*) or border settlement (*Scots Gaelic*), used as a first name (*Old English*).

Crépin *masc* the French form of **Crispin**.

Cressida *fem* gold (*Greek*); a contracted form is **Cressa**.

Crispin, Crispian *masc* having curly hair (*Latin*).

Crispus *masc* the German form of **Crispin**.

Cristal *fem* a variant form of **Crystal**.

Cristiano *masc* the Italian and Spanish form of **Christian**.

Cristina *fem* the Italian, Portuguese and Spanish form of **Christina**.

Cristóbal *masc* the Spanish form of **Christopher**.

Cristoforo *masc* the Italian form of **Christopher**.

Cromwell *masc* a placename and surname, meaning winding spring, used as a first name.

Crosbie, Crosby *masc* a placename and surname, meaning farm or village with crosses, used as a first name (*Old Norse*).

Crystal *fem* the name of a very clear brilliant glass used as a first name; variant forms are **Cristal, Chrystal**.

Cullan, Cullen *masc* a surname, meaning Cologne, used as a first name (*Old French*); a placename, meaning at the back of the river, used as a first name (*Scots Gaelic*).

Culley *masc* a surname, meaning woodland, used as a
first name (*Scots Gaelic*).

Curran *masc* a surname, of uncertain meaning—
possibly resolute hero, used as a first name (*Irish
Gaelic*).

Curt *masc* a variant form of **Kurt**; a diminutive form
of **Curtis**.

Curtis *masc* a surname, meaning courteous, educated,
used as a first name (*Old French*); a diminutive form
is **Curt**.

Cuthbert *masc* famous bright (*Old English*).

Cy *masc* a diminutive form of **Cyrus**.

Cynthia *fem* belonging to Mount Cynthus (*Greek*);
diminutive forms are **Cindie, Cindy**.

Cyprian *masc* from Cyprus, the Mediterranean island
(*Greek*).

Cyrano *masc* from Cyrene, an ancient city of North
Africa (*Greek*).

Cyrene, Cyrena *fem* from Cyrene, an ancient city of
North Africa; in Greek mythology, a water nymph
loved by Apollo (*Greek*); a variant form is **Kyrena**.

Cyril *masc* lordly (*Greek*).

Cyrill *masc* the German form of **Cyril**.

Cyrille *masc* the French form of Cyril; *fem* form of
Cyril (*French*).

Cyrillus *masc* the Danish, Dutch and Swedish forms of
Cyril.

Cyrus *masc* the sun (*Persian*); a diminutive form is **Cy**.

Cytherea *fem* from Cythera, an island off the southern coast of the Peloponnese, in Greek mythology, home of a cult of Aphrodite (*Greek*).

Cythereia *fem* from Cytherea, in Greek mythology, an alternative name for Aphrodite.

D

Daffodil *fem* the name of the spring plant that yields bright yellow flowers used as a first name (*Dutch/ Latin*); a diminutive form is **Daffy**.

Dafydd *masc* a Welsh form of **David**.

Dag *masc* day (*Norse*).

Dagan *masc* earth, the name of an earth god of the Assyrians and Babylonians (*Semitic*).

Dagmar *fem* bright day (*Norse*).

Dahlia *fem* the name of the plant with brightly coloured flowers, named after the Swedish botanist Anders Dahl (dale), used as a first name.

Dai *masc* a Welsh diminutive form of David, formerly a name in its own right, meaning shining.

Daisy *fem* the name of the plant; the day's eye (*Old English*).

Dale *masc fem* a surname, meaning valley, used as a first name (*Old English*).

Daley *masc, fem* a surname, meaning assembly, used as a first name (*Irish Gaelic*); a variant form is **Daly**.

Dalilah, Dalila *fem* variant forms of **Delilah**.

Dallas *masc* a surname, meaning meadow resting place (*Scots Gaelic*) or dale house (*Old English*), used as a first name.

Dalton *masc* a surname, meaning dale farm, used as a first name (*Old English*).

Daly *masc, fem* a variant of **Daley**.

Dalziel *masc* a placename and surname, meaning field of the sungleam, used as a first name (*Scots Gaelic*).

Damian *masc* the French form of **Damon**.

Damiano *masc* the Italian form of **Damon**.

Damien *masc* taming (*Greek*).

Damon *masc* conqueror (*Greek*).

Dan *masc* a diminutive form of **Danby, Daniel**.

Dana *masc, fem* a surname, of uncertain meaning—possibly Danish, used as a first name (*Old English*); *fem* form of **Dan, Daniel**.

Danaë *fem* in Greek mythology, the mother of Perseus by Zeus, who came to her as shower of gold while she was in prison; diminutive forms are **Dannie, Danny**.

Danby *masc* a placename and surname, meaning Danes' settlement, used as a first name (*Old Norse*); a diminutive form is **Dan**.

Dandie *masc* a Scottish diminutive form of **Andrew**.

Dane *masc* a surname, meaning valley, used as a first name (*Old English*).

Daniel *masc* God is my judge (*Hebrew*); diminutive

forms are **Dan, Dannie, Danny**.

Danielle *fem* form of **Daniel**; *masc* the Italian form of
Daniel.

Dannie, Danny *masc* diminutives of **Danby, Daniel**;
fem diminutives of **Danaë, Danielle**.

Dante *masc* steadfast (*Latin/Italian*).

Daphne *fem* laurel (*Greek*).

Dara *fem* charity (*Hebrew*); *masc* oak (*Irish Gaelic*).

Darby *masc* a variant form of Derby, a surname
meaning a village where deer are seen, used as a
surname (*Old Norse*); a diminutive form of **Dermot,
Diarmid** (*Irish Gaelic*).

Darcie *fem* form of **Darcy**.

Darcy, D'Arcy *masc* a surname, meaning fortress, used
as a first name (*Old French*).

Darell *masc* a variant form of **Darrell**.

Daria *fem* form of **Darius**.

Darien *masc* a South American placename used as a
first name.

Dario *masc* the Italian form of **Darius**.

Darius *masc* preserver (*Persian*).

Darlene, Darleen *fem* the endearment 'darling' com-
bined with a suffix to form a first name (*Old English*).

Darnell *masc* a surname, meaning hidden nook, used as
a first name (*Old English*).

Darrell, Darrel *masc* from a surname, meaning from

Airelle in Normandy, used as a first name; variant
forms are **Darell, Darryl, Daryl**.

Darrelle *fem* form of Darrell (*French*).

Darren, Darin *masc* a surname, of unknown origin,
used as a first name.

Darryl a variant form of **Darrell**, also used as a girl's
name.

Darton *masc* a surname, meaning deer enclosure or
forest, used as a first name (*Old English*).

Daryl a variant form of **Darrell**, also used as a girl's
name.

David *masc* beloved (*Hebrew*); diminutive forms are
Dave, Davie, Davy.

Davidde *masc* the Italian form of David.

Davide *masc* the French form of **David**.

Davie *masc* a diminutive form of **David**.

Davin *masc* a variant form of **Devin**.

Davina *fem* form of **David**.

Davis *masc* David's son (*Old English*).

Davy *masc* a diminutive form of **David**.

Dawn *fem* the name of the first part of the day used as a
personal name (*English*).

Dean *masc* a surname, meaning one who lives in a
valley (*Old English*) or serving as a dean (*Old French*),
used as a first name; the anglicized form of **Dino**.

Deana, Deane *fem* forms of Dean; variant forms are
Dena, Dene.

Deanna *fem* a variant form of **Diana**.

Dearborn *masc* a surname, meaning deer brook, used as a first name (*Old English*).

Deborah, Debra *fem* bee (*Hebrew*); diminutive forms are **Deb, Debbie, Debby**.

Decima *fem* form of Decimus.

Decimus *masc* tenth (*Latin*).

Declan *masc* the name, of unknown meaning, of a 5th-century Irish saint (*Irish Gaelic*).

Dedrick *masc* people's ruler (*Germanic*).

Dee *fem* a diminutive form of names beginning with D.

Deinol *masc* charming (*Welsh*).

Deirdre *fem* meaning uncertain, possibly sorrowful (*Irish Gaelic*).

Delfine *fem* a variant form of **Delphine**.

Delia *fem* woman of Delos (*Greek*).

Delicia *fem* great delight (*Latin*).

Delight *fem* the abstract noun for great pleasure, satisfaction or joy used as a first name (*Old French*).

Delilah, Delila *fem* meaning uncertain, possibly delicate (*Hebrew*); a variant forms are **Dalila, Dalilah**; a diminutive form is **Lila**.

Dell *masc* a surname, meaning one who lives in a hollow, used as a first name; a diminutive form of **Delmar**, etc.

Delma *fem* form of **Delmar**; a diminutive form of **Fidelma**.

Delmar *masc* of the sea (*Latin*).

Delores *fem* a variant form of **Dolores**.

Delphine *fem* dolphin (*Latin*); a variant form is **Delfine**.

Delwyn, Delwin *masc* neat and blessed (*Welsh*).

Delyth *fem* pretty (*Welsh*).

Demetria *fem* form of **Demeter**.

Demetre *masc* the French form of **Demetrius**.

Demetrio *masc* the Italian form of **Demetrius**.

Demetrius *masc* belonging to Demeter, goddess of the
harvest, earth mother (*Greek*).

Dempsey *masc* a surname, meaning proud descendant,
used as a first name (*Gaelic*).

Dempster *masc* a surname, meaning judge, used as a
first name, formerly a feminine one (*Old English*).

Den *masc* diminutive form of **Denis, Dennis, Denison,
Denley, Denman, Dennison, Denton, Denver,
Denzel, Denzell, Denzil**.

Dena, Dene *fem* variant forms of **Deana**.

Denby *masc* a surname, meaning Danish settlement,
used as a first name (*Norse*).

Denice *fem* a variant form of **Denise**.

Denis, Dennis *masc* belonging to Dionysus, the god of
wine (*Greek*).

Denise *fem* form of **Denis**; a variant form is **Denice**.

Denison *masc* a variant form of **Dennison**.

Denley *masc* a surname, meaning wood or clearing in a
valley, used as a first name (*Old English*).

Denman *masc* a surname, meaning dweller in a valley, used as a first name (*Old English*).

Dennison *masc* son of Dennis (*Old English*); variant forms are **Denison, Tennison, Tennyson**.

Denton *masc* a surname, meaning valley place, used as a first name (*Old English*).

Denver *masc* a surname, meaning Danes' crossing, used as a first name (*Old English*).

Denzel, Denzell, Denzil *masc* a surname, meaning stronghold, used as a first name (*Celtic*).

Deon *masc* a variant form of **Dion**.

Derek, *masc* an English form of **Theoderic**; variant forms are **Derrick, Derrik**; a diminutive form is **Derry**.

Dermot *masc* the anglicized form of **Diarmaid**; a diminutive form is **Derry**.

Derrick, Derrik *masc* variant forms of **Derek**; a diminutive form is **Derry**.

Derry *masc* the anglicized form of a placename, meaning oak wood, used as a first name (*Irish Gaelic*); a diminutive form of **Derek, Derrick, Derrik, Dermot**.

Derwent *masc* a placename and surname, meaning river that flows through oak woods, used as a first name (*Old English*).

Desdemona *fem* ill-fated (*Greek*), the name given by Shakespeare to the wife of Othello.

Desirée *fem* longed for (*French*).

Desmond *masc* a varient form of **Esmond** (*Germanic*).

Deverell, Deverill *masc* a surname, meaning fertile river bank, used as a first name (*Celtic*).

Devin, Devinn *masc* a surname, meaning poet, used as a first name (*Irish Gaelic*); a variant form is **Davin**.

Devlin *masc* fiercely brave (*Irish Gaelic*).

Devon *masc* the name of the English county, meaning deep ones, used as a first name (*Celtic*)

Devona *fem* form of **Devon**.

Dewey *masc* a Celtic form of **David**.

Dewi *masc* a Welsh form of **David**.

De Witt *masc* fair-haired (*Flemish*).

Dexter *masc* a surname, meaning (woman) dyer, used as a first name (*Old English*).

Di *fem* a diminutive form of **Diana, Diane, Dianne, Dina, Dinah**.

Diamond *masc* the name of the gem, meaning the hardest iron or steel, used as a first name (*Latin*).

Diana *fem* goddess (*Latin*); a diminutive form is **Di**.

Diane, Dianne *fem* French forms of **Diana**.

Diarmaid *masc* free of envy (*Irish Gaelic*); a variant form is **Diarmuid**; the anglized form is **Dermot**.

Diarmid *masc* the Scottish Gaelic form of **Diarmaid**.

Diarmuid *masc* a variant form of **Diarmaid**.

Dick, Dickie, Dickon *masc* diminutive forms of **Richard**.

Dickson *masc* a surname, meaning son of Richard, used
    as a first name (*Old English*); a variant form is
    Dixon.

Dicky *masc* a diminutive form of **Richard**.

Dido *fem* teacher (*Greek*), in Greek mythology a
    princess from Tyre who founded Carthage and
    became its queen.

Diego *masc* a Spanish form of **James**.

Dietrich *masc* the German form of **Derek**; a diminutive
    form is Till.

Digby *masc* a surname, meaning settlement at a ditch,
    used as a first name (*Old Norse*).

Dillon *masc* a surname of uncertain meaning, possibly
    destroyer, used as a first name (*Germanic/Irish
    Gaelic*).

Dilys *fem* sure, genuine (*Welsh*); a diminutive form is
    Dilly.

Dina *fem* form of **Dino**; a variant form of **Dinah**.

Dinah *fem* vindicated (*Hebrew*); a variant form is **Dina**;
    a diminutive form is **Di**.

Dino *masc* a diminutive ending, indicating little, now
    used independently (*Italian*).

Dion *masc* a shortened form of Dionysus, the god of
    wine (*Greek*); a variant form is **Deon**.

Dione, Dionne *fem* daughter of heaven and earth
    (*Greek*), in Greek mythology the earliest consort of
    Zeus and mother of Aphrodite.

Dirk *masc* the Dutch form of **Derek**; a diminutive form of **Theodoric**.

Dixie *fem* a diminutive form of Benedicta.

Dixon *masc* a variant form of **Dickson**.

Dodie, Dodo *fem* diminutive forms of **Dorothy**.

Dolan *masc* a variant form of **Doolan**.

Dolina *fem* a Scottish diminutive form of **Donalda**.

Dolly *fem* a diminutive form of **Dorothy**.

Dolores *fem* sorrows (*Spanish*); a variant form is **Delores**; diminutive forms are **Lola, Lolita**.

Dolph *masc* a diminutive form of **Adolph**.

Domenico *masc* the Italian form of **Dominic**.

Domingo *masc* the Spanish form of **Dominic**.

Dominic, Dominick *masc* belonging to the lord (*Latin*); a diminutive form is **Dom**.

Dominique *masc* the French form of **Dominic**, now used in English as a girl's name.

Don *masc* a diminutive form of **Donal, Donald, Donall**.

Dónal *masc* an Irish Gaelic form of **Donald**.

Donal *masc* anglicized forms of **Dónal**; a variant form is **Donall**; diminutive forms are **Don, Donnie, Donny**.

Donald *masc* proud chief (*Scots Gaelic*); diminutive forms are **Don, Donnie, Donny**.

Donalda *fem* form. of **Donald**.

Donall *masc* a variant form of **Donal**.

Donata *fem* form of **Donato**.

Donato *masc* gift of God (*Latin*).

Donna *fem* lady (*Italian*).

Donnie, Donny *masc* diminutive forms of **Donal, Donald, Donall**.

Doolan *masc* a surname, meaning black defiance, used as a first name (*Irish Gaelic*); a variant form is **Dolan**.

Dora *fem* a diminutive form of **Dorothea, Theodora**, etc, now used independently; diminutive forms are **Dorrie, Dorry**.

Doran *masc* a surname, meaning stranger or exile, used as a first name (*Irish Gaelic*).

Dorcas *fem* a gazelle (*Greek*).

Doreen *fem* an Irish variant form of **Dora**.

Dorian *masc* Dorian man, one of a Hellenic people who invaded Greece in the 2nd century BC (*Greek*); its use as a first name was probably invented by Oscar Wilde for his novel, *The Picture of Dorian Gray*.

Dorinda *fem* lovely gift (*Greek*); diminutive forms are **Dorrie, Dorry**.

Doris *fem* Dorian woman, one of a Hellenic people who invaded Greece in the 2nd century BC (*Greek*); diminutive forms are **Dorrie, Dorry**.

Dorothea *fem* a German form of **Dorothea**; a diminutive form is **Thea**.

Dorothée *fem* a French form of **Dorothea**.

Dorothy *fem* the gift of God (*Greek*); diminutive forms are **Dodie, Dodo, Dolly, Dot**.

Dorrie, Dorry *fem* diminutive forms of **Dora, Dorinda, Doris**.

Dorward *masc* a variant form of **Durward**.

Dougal, Dougall *masc* black stranger (*Gaelic*); variant forms are **Dugal, Dugald**; diminutive forms are **Doug, Dougie, Duggie**.

Douglas *masc fem* a placename, meaning black water, used as a first name (*Scots Gaelic*); diminutive forms are **Doug, Dougie, Duggie**.

Dow *masc* a surname, meaning black or black-haired, used as a first name (*Scots Gaelic*).

Doyle *masc* an Irish Gaelic form of **Dougal**.

D'Oyley *masc* a surname, meaning from Ouilly—rich land, used as a first name (*Old French*).

Drake *masc* a surname, meaning dragon or standard bearer, used as a first name (*Old English*).

Drew *masc* a diminutive form of **Andrew**; a surname, meaning trusty (*Germanic*) or lover (*Old French*) used as a first name.

Driscoll, Driscol *masc* a surname, meaning interpreter, used as a first name (*Irish Gaelic*).

Druce *masc* a surname, meaning from Eure or Rieux in France (*Old French*), or sturdy lover, used as a first name (*Celtic*).

Drummond *masc* a surname, meaning ridge, used as a first name.

Drury *masc* a surname, meaning dear one, used as a first name (*Old French*).

Drusilla *fem* with dewy eyes (*Latin*).

Dryden *masc* a surname, meaning dry valley, used as a first name (*Old English*).

Duane *masc* dark (*Irish Gaelic*); variant forms are **Dwane, Dwayne**.

Dudley *masc* a placename, meaning Dudda's clearing, used as a first name (*Old English*).

Duff *masc* a surname, meaning black- or dark-complexioned, used as a first name (*Scots Gaelic*).

Dugal, Dugald *masc* variant forms of **Dougal**; a diminutive form is **Duggie**.

Duggie *masc* a diminutive form of **Dougal, Dougald, Douglas, Dugal, Dugald**.

Duke *masc* the title of an English aristocrat used as a first name; a diminutive form of **Marmaduke**.

Dulcie *fem* a diminutive form of **Dulcibella**, meaning sweet beautiful (*Latin*).

Duncan *masc* brown chief (*Gaelic*); a diminutive form is **Dunc**.

Dunlop *masc* a surname, meaning muddy hill, used as a first name (*Scots Gaelic*).

Dunn, Dunne *masc* a surname, meaning dark-skinned, used as a first name (*Old English*).

Dunstan *masc* brown hill stone (*Old English*).

Durand, Durant *masc* a surname, meaning enduring or obstinate, used as a first name (*Old French*).

Durward *masc* a surname, meaning doorkeeper or gatekeeper, used as a first name (*Old English*); a variant form is **Dorward**.

Durwin *masc* Dear friend *Old English*); a diminutive form is **Durwyn**.

Dustin *masc* a surname, of uncertain meaning—possibly of Dionysus, used as a first name.

Dwane, Dwayne *masc* variant forms of **Duane**.

Dwight *masc* a surname, meaning Thor's stone, used as a first name (*Old Norse*).

Dyan *fem* a variant form of **Diane**.

Dyfan *masc* ruler (*Welsh*).

Dylan *masc* sea (*Welsh*).

Dymphna *fem* little fawn (*Irish Gaelic*).

E

Eachan, Eachann, Eacheann *masc* horse (*Scots Gaelic*).

Eamon, Eamonn *masc* an Irish Gaelic form of **Edmund**.

Éanna bird (*Irish Gaelic*); an anglicized form is **Enda**.

Earl, Earle *masc* an English title, meaning nobleman, used as a first name (*Old English*); a variant form is **Erle**.

Earlene, Earline *fem* form.of **Earl**; variant forms are **Erlene, Erline**; diminutive forms are **Earlie, Earley**.

Eartha *fem* of the earth (*Old English*); a variant form is **Ertha**.

Easter *fem* the name of the Christian festival, used as a first name.

Eaton masc a surname, meaning river or island farm, used as a first name (*Old English*).

Ebba *fem* wild boar (*Germanic*); an Old English form of **Eve**.

Eben *masc* stone (*Hebrew*); a diminutive form is **Eb**.

Ebenezer *masc* stone of help (*Hebrew*); diminutive forms are **Eb, Eben**.

Eberhard, Ebert *masc* German forms of **Everard**.

Ebony *fem* the name of the dark hard wood used as a first name.

Echo *fem* the name for the physical phenomenon of the reflection of sound or other radiation used as a first name; in Greek mythology it is the name of the nymph who pined away for love of Narcissus.

Ed *masc* a diminutive form of **Edbert, Edgar, Edmund, Edward, Edwin**.

Eda *fem* prosperity, happiness (*Old English*).

Edan *masc* a Scottish form of **Aidan**.

Edana *fem* form of **Edan**.

Edbert *masc* prosperous; bright (*Old English*).

Eddie, Eddy *masc* diminutive forms of **Edbert, Edgar, Edmund, Edward, Edwin**.

Edel *masc* noble (*Germanic*).

Edelmar *masc* noble, famous (*Old English*)

Eden *masc* pleasantness (*Hebrew*); a surname, meaning blessed helmet, used as a first name.

Edgar *masc* prosperity spear (*Old English*); diminutive forms are **Ed, Eddie, Eddy, Ned, Neddie, Neddy**.

Edie *fem* a diminutive form of **Edina, Edith, Edwina**.

Edina *fem* a Scottish variant form of **Edwina**.

Edith *fem* prosperity strife (*Old English*); variant forms are **Edyth, Edythe**; diminutive forms are **Edie, Edy**.

Edlyn *fem* noble maid (*Old English*).

Edmond *masc* the French form of **Edmund**.

Edmonda *fem* form of Edmund (*Old English*).

Edmund *masc* prosperity defender (*Old English*).

Edna *fem* pleasure (*Hebrew*).

Edoardo *masc* an Italian form of **Edward**.

Édouard *masc* the French form of **Edward**.

Edrea *fem* form of **Edric**.

Edric *masc* wealthy ruler (*Old English*).

Edryd *masc* restoration (*Welsh*).

Edsel *masc* noble (*Germanic*).

Eduardo *masc* the Italian and Spanish form of **Edward**.

Edwald *masc* prosperous ruler (*Old English*).

Edward *masc* guardian of happiness (*Old English*); diminutive forms are **Ed, Eddie, Eddy, Ned, Ted, Teddy**.

Edwardina *fem* form of **Edward**.

Edwige *fem* the French form of **Hedwig**.

Edwin *masc* prosperity friend (*Old English*).

Edwina *fem* form of **Edwin**; a variant form is **Edina**.

Edy *fem* a diminutive form of **Edith**.

Edyth, Edythe *fem* variant forms of **Edith**.

Effie *fem* a diminutive form of **Euphemia**.

Egan *masc* a surname, meaning son of Hugh, used as a first name (*Irish Gaelic*).

Egbert *masc* sword bright (*Germanic*).

Egberta *fem* form of Egbert (*Old English*).

Egidio *masc* the Italian and Spanish form of **Giles**.

Eglantine *fem* an alternative name for the wild rose, meaning sharp, keen, used as a first name (*Old French*).

Ehren *masc* Honourable one (*Germanic*).

Eileen *fem* the Irish form of **Helen**; a variant form is **Aileen**.

Eilidh *fem* a Scots Gaelic form of **Helen**.

Eilir *masc* butterfly (*Welsh*).

Einar *masc* single warrior (*Old Norse*).

Eira *fem* snow (*Welsh*).

Eirlys *fem* snowdrop (*Welsh*).

Eithne *fem* kernel (*Irish Gaelic*); anglicized forms are **Ena, Ethna**.

Elaine *fem* a French form of **Helen**.

Elder *masc* a surname, meaning senior, elder, used as a first name (*Old English*).

Eldon *masc* a surname, meaning Ella's hill, used as a first name (*Old English*).

Eldora *fem* a shortened form of El Dorado, meaning the land of gold, used as a first name (*Spanish*).

Eldred *masc* terrible (*Old English*).

Eldrida *fem* form.of **Eldrid**.

Eldrid, Eldridge *masc* wise adviser (*Old English*).

Eleanor, Eleanore *fem* variant forms of **Helen**; a variant form is **Elinor**; diminutive forms are **Ella, Nell, Nora**.

Eleanora *fem* the Italian form of **Eleanor**.

Eleazer *masc* a variant form of **Eliezer**.

Electra *fem* brilliant (*Greek*).

Elen *fem* angel, nymph (*Welsh*).

Elena *fem* the Italian and Spanish form of **Helen**.

Eleonora *fem* the Italian form of **Eleanor**.

Eleonore *fem* the German form of **Eleanor**.

Eléonore *fem* a French form of **Leonora**.

Elfed *masc* autumn (*Welsh*).

Elfleda *fem* noble beauty (*Old English*).

Elfreda *fem* elf strength (*Old English*).

Elga *fem* holy (*Old Norse*); a variant form of **Olga**.

Elgan *masc* bright circle (*Welsh*).

Eli *masc* a diminutive form of **Elias, Elijah, Eliezer**; a variant form is **Ely**.

Elias *masc* a variant form of **Elijah**; a diminutive form is **Eli**.

Eliezer *masc* my God is help (*Hebrew*); a variant form is **Eleazar**.

Elihu *masc* he is my God (*Hebrew*).

Elijah *masc* Jehovah is my God (*Hebrew*); a diminutive form is **Lije**.

Elin *fem* a Welsh diminutive form of **Elinor**; a Welsh variant form of **Helen**.

Elinor *fem* a variant form of **Eleanor**.

Eliot *masc* a variant form of **Elliot**.

Elis *masc* a Welsh form of **Elias**.

Elisa *fem* an Italian diminutive form of **Elisabetta**.

Elisabeth *fem* a French and German form of **Elizabeth**.

Elisabetta *fem* an Italian form of **Elizabeth**.

Élise *fem* a French diminutive form of **Elisabeth**.

Elisha *masc* God is salvation (*Hebrew*).

Elizabeth *fem* worshiper of God; consecrated to God (*Hebrew*); diminutive forms are **Bess, Bet, Beth, Betsy, Betty, Eliza, Elsa, Elsie, Libby, Lisa, Liza, Lisbeth, Liz**.

Ella *fem* a diminutive form of **Cinderella, Eleanor, Isabella**.

Ellen *fem* a variant form of **Helen**.

Ellice *fem* form of **Elias, Ellis**.

Ellie *fem* a diminutive form of **Alice**.

Elliot, Elliot *masc* a surname, from a French diminutive form of Elias, used as a first name.

Ellis *masc* a surname, a Middle English form of **Elias**, used as a first name.

Ellison *masc* a surname, meaning son of Elias, used as a first name (*Old English*).

Elma *fem* a diminutive form of **Wilhelmina**; a contracted form of **Elizabeth Mary**.

Elmer *masc* noble; excellent (*Germanic*)

Elmo *masc* amiable (*Greek*).

Elmore *masc* a surname, meaning river bank with elms, used as a first name (*Old English*).

Éloise, Eloisa *fem* sound, whole (*Germanic*); a variant form is **Héloïse**.

Elroy *masc* a variant form of **Leroy**.

Elsa *fem* a diminutive form of **Alison, Alice, Elizabeth**.

Elsie *fem* a diminutive form of **Alice, Alison, Elizabeth, Elspeth**.

Elspeth, Elspet *fem* Scottish forms of **Elizabeth**;
diminutive forms are **Elsie, Elspie**.

Elton *masc* a surname, meaning settlement of Ella,
used as a first name (*Old English*).

Eluned *fem* idol (*Welsh*).

Elva *fem* friend of the elf (*Old English*); a variant form
is **Elvina**.

Elvey *masc* a surname, meaning elf gift, used as a first
name (*Old English*); a variant form is **Elvy**.

Elvin *masc* a surname, meaning elf or noble friend,
used as a first name (*Old English*); a variant form is
Elwin.

Elvina *fem* a variant form of **Elva**.

Elvira *fem* white (*Latin*).

Elvis *masc* wise one (*Norse*).

Elvy *masc* a variant form of **Elvey**.

Elwin *masc* a variant form of **Elvin**; white brow
(*Welsh*); a variant form is **Elwyn**.

Emanuel *masc* God with us (*Hebrew*); a variant form is
Immanuel; a diminutive form is **Manny**.

Emeline *fem* a variant form of **Amelia**; a diminutive
form of **Emma**; a variant form is **Emmeline**.

Emerald *fem* the name of the green gemstone used as a
first name.

Emery *masc* a variant form of **Amory**.

Emil *masc* of a noble Roman family the origin of whose name, *Aemilius*, is uncertain.

Émile *masc* the French form of **Emil**.

Emilia *fem* the Italian form of **Emily**.

Emilie *fem* the German form of **Emily**.

Émilie *fem* the French form of **Emily**.

Emilio *masc* the Italian, Spanish and Portuguese form of **Emil**.

Emily *fem* of a noble Roman family the origin of whose name, *Aemilius*, is uncertain.

Emlyn *masc* origin uncertain, possibly from **Emil** (*Welsh*).

Emma *fem* whole, universal (*Germanic*); diminutive forms are **Emm**, **Emmie**.

Emmeline *fem* a variant form of **Emeline**.

Emery m*asc* a variant form of **Amory**.

Emmet, Emmett, Emmot, Emmott *masc* a surname, from a diminutive form of Emma, used as a first name.

Emory *masc* a variant form of **Amory**.

Emrys *masc* a Welsh form of **Ambrose**.

Emyr *masc* a Welsh form of **Honorius**.

Ena *fem* an anglicized form of **Eithne**.

Enda *fem* an anglicized form of **Éanna**.

Eneas *masc* a variant form of **Aeneas**.

Enée *masc* the French form of **Aeneas**.

Enfys *fem* rainbow (*Welsh*).

Engelbert *masc* bright angel (*Germanic*).

Engelberta, Engelbertha, Engelberthe *fem* forms of
   Engelbert.

Enid *fem* meaning uncertain, possibly
   woodlark(*Welsh*).

Ennis *masc* chief one (*Gaelic*).

Enoch *masc* dedication (*Hebrew*).

Enos *masc* man (*Hebrew*).

Enrica *fem* the Italian form of **Henrietta**.

Enrichetta *fem* the Italian form of **Henrietta**.

Enrico *masc* the Italian form of **Henry**.

Enrique *masc* the Spanish form of **Henry**.

Enriqueta *fem* the Spanish form of **Henrietta**.

Eoghan *masc* an Irish Gaelic form of **Eugene**.

Eoin *masc* an Irish form of **John**.

Ephraim *masc* fruitful (*Hebrew*); a diminutive form is
   Eph.

Eranthe *fem* flower of spring (*Greek*).

Erasmus *masc* lovely; worthy of love (*Greek*); a
   diminutive form is **Ras, Rasmus**.

Erastus *masc* beloved (*Greek*); diminutive forms are
   Ras, Rastus.

Ercole *masc* the Italian form of **Hercules**.

Erda *fem* of the earth (*Germanic*).

Eric *masc* rich; brave; powerful (*Old English*); a
   variant form is **Erik**.

Erica *fem* form of **Eric**; a variant form is **Erika**.

Erich *masc* the German form of **Eric**.

Erik *masc* a variant form of **Eric**.

Erika *fem* a variant form of **Erica**.

Erin *fem* the poetic name for Ireland used as a first name.

Erland *masc* stranger (*Old Norse*).

Erle *masc* a variant form of **Earl**.

Erlene, Erline *fem* variant forms of **Earlene, Erline**; diminutive forms are **Erlie, Erley**.

Erma *fem* warrior maid (*Germanic*).

Ern *masc* a diminutive form of **Ernest**.

Erna *fem* a diminutive form of **Ernesta, Ernestine**.

Ernest *masc* earnestness (*Germanic*); diminutive forms are **Ern, Ernie**.

Ernesta *fem* form of **Ernest**; a diminutive form is **Erna**.

Ernestine *fem* form of **Ernest**; diminutive forms are **Erna, Tina**.

Ernesto *masc* the Italian and Spanish forms of **Ernest**.

Ernst *masc* the German form of **Ernest**.

Erskine *masc* a placename and surname, meaning projecting height, used as a first name (*Scots Gaelic*).

Erwin *masc* friend of honour (*Germanic*); a surname, meaning wild-boar friend (*French*), used as a first name; a variant form is **Orwin**.

Eryl *masc* watcher (*Welsh*).

Esau *masc* hairy (*Hebrew*).

Esmé *masc, fem* beloved (*French*).

Esmeralda *fem* a Spanish form of **Emerald**.

Esmond *masc* divine protection (*Old English*).

Esta *fem* a variant form of **Esther**.

Este *masc* Man from the East (*Italian*).

Estéban *masc* the Spanish form of **Stephen**.

Estelle, Estella *fem* variant forms of **Stella**.

Ester *fem* the Italian and Spanish forms of **Esther**.

Esther *fem* the planet Venus (*Persian*); a variant form is
    Esta; diminutive forms are **Ess, Essie, Tess, Tessie**.

Estrella *fem* the Spanish form of **Estelle**.

Ethan *masc* firm (*Hebrew*).

Ethel *fem* noble; of noble birth (*Old English*).

Ethna *fem* an anglicized form of **Eithne**.

Etienne *masc* the French form of **Stephen**.

Etta, Ettie *fem* diminutive forms of **Henrietta**.

Ettore *masc* the Italian form of **Hector**.

Euan *masc* a variant form of **Ewan**.

Eudora *fem* good gift (*Greek*).

Eufemia *fem* the Italian and Spanish form of
    Euphemia.

Eugen *masc* the German form of **Eugene**.

Eugene *masc* well-born; noble (*Greek*); a diminutive
    form is **Gene**.

Eugène *masc* the French form of **Eugene**.

Eugenia *fem* form of **Eugene**; diminutive forms are
    Ena, Gene.

Eugénie *fem* the French form of **Eugenia**.

Eulalie*fem* fair speech (*Greek*).

Eunice *fem* good victory (*Greek*).

Euphemia *fem* of good report (*Greek*); diminutive forms are **Fay, Effie, Phamie, Phemie**.

Eurig, Euros *masc* gold (*Welsh*).

Eusebio *masc* pious (*Greek*).

Eustace *masc* rich (*Greek*); diminutive forms are **Stacey, Stacy**.

Eustache *masc* the French form of **Eustace**.

Eustachio *masc* the Italian form of **Eustace**.

Eustacia *fem* form of **Eustace**; diminutive forms are **Stacey, Stacie, Stacy**.

Eustaquio *masc* the Spanish form of **Eustace**.

Eva *fem* the German, Italian, and Spanish forms of **Eve**.

Evadne *fem* of uncertain meaning, possibly high-born (*Greek*).

Evan *masc* young warrior (*Celtic*).

Evangeline *fem* of the Gospel (*Greek*).

Eve *fem* life (*Hebrew*); diminutive forms are **Evie, Evelina, Eveline, Eveleen**.

Eveline *fem* a diminutive form of **Eva, Eve**.

Evelyn *masc fem* the English surname used as a first name.

Everard *masc* strong boar (*Germanic*).

Everley *masc* Field of the wild boar (*Old English*).

Evita *fem* Spanish diminutive form of **Eva**.

Evodia *fem* good journey (*Greek*).

Ewan, Ewen *masc* Irish and Scots Gaelic forms of **Owen**; a Scottish form of **Eugene**; a variant form is **Euan**.

Ewart *masc* an Old French variant of **Edward**; a surname, meaning herd of ewes used as a surname(*Old English*).

Ezekiel *masc* strength of God (*Hebrew*); a diminutive form is **Zeke**.

Ezra *masc* help (*Hebrew*).

F

Fabia *fem* form of **Fabio**; a variant form is **Fabiola**.

Fabian *masc* the anglicized form of the Roman family name *Fabianus*, derived from *Fabius*, from *faba*, bean (*Latin*).

Fabián *masc* the Spanish form of **Fabian**.

Fabiano *masc* the Italian form of **Fabian**.

Fabien *masc* the French form of **Fabian**.

Fabienne *fem* form of **Fabien**.

Fabio *masc* the Italian form of the Roman family name *Fabius*, from *faba*, bean.

Fabiola *fem* a variant form of **Fabia**.

Faber, Fabre *masc* a surname, meaning smith, used as a first name (*Latin*).

Fabrice *masc* the French form of the Roman family *Fabricius*, from *faber*, smith.

Fabrizio *masc* the Italian form of **Fabrice**.

Fairfax *masc* the surname, meaning lovely hair, used as a first name (*Old English*).

Fairley, Fairlie *masc* a surname, meaning clearing with ferns, used as a first name (*Old English*).

Faith *fem* the quality of belief or fidelity used as a first name.

Fanchon *fem* a diminutive form of **Françoise**.

Fane *masc* a surname, meaning glad or eager, used as a first name (*Old English*).

Fanny *fem* a diminutive form of **Frances**, also used independently.

Farnall, Farnell *masc* a surname, meaning fern hill, used as a first name(*Old English*); variant forms are **Fernald, Fernall**.

Farquhar *masc* dear man (*Scots Gaelic*).

Farr *masc* a surname, meaning bull, used as a first name (*Old English*).

Farrell *masc* warrior (*Irish Gaelic*).

Faustina, Faustine *fem* lucky (*Latin*).

Fatima *fem* the name of the daughter of Mohammed (*Semitic*); of Fatima in Portugal (*Portuguese*).

Favor, Favour *fem* an abstract noun, meaning good will or an act of good will, from *favere*, to protect, used as a first name (*Latin*).

Fawn *fem* the name for a young deer or a light greyish-brown colour used as a first name (*Old French*).

Fay, Faye *fem* faith or fairy (*Old French*); a diminutive form of **Euphemia**.

Federico *masc* an Italian and Spanish form of **Frederick**.

Felice *masc* the Italian form of **Felix**.

Felicia *fem* form of **Felix**.

Felicidad *fem* the Spanish form of **Felicia**.

Felicie *fem* the Italian form of **Felicia**.

Felicity *fem* happiness (*Latin*).

Felipe *masc* the Spanish form of **Philip**.

Felix *masc* happy (*Latin*).

Felton *masc* a placename and surname, meaning place in a field, used as a first name (*Old English*).

Fenella *fem* an anglicized form of **Fionnuala**.

Fenton *masc* a placename and surname, meaning a place in marshland or fens, used as a first name (*Old English*).

Ferdinand *masc* peace bold (*Germanic*); diminutive forms are **Ferd, Ferdy**.

Ferdinando *masc* an Italian form of **Ferdinand**.

Fergal *masc* man of strength (*Irish Gaelic*); diminutive forms are **Fergie, Fergy**.

Fergie *masc* a diminutive form of **Fergal, Fergus, Ferguson**; *fem* a diminutive form of **Ferguson** as a surname; a variant form is **Fergy**.

Fergus *masc* vigorous man (*Irish/Scots Gaelic*); diminutive forms are **Fergie, Fergy**.

Ferguson, Fergusson *masc* a surname, meaning son of Fergus, used as a first name; diminutive forms are **Fergie, Fergy**.

Fergy *masc*, *fem* a variant form of **Fergie**.

Fern *fem* the name of the plant used as a first name (*Old English*).

Fernald, Fernall *masc* variant forms of **Farnall, Farnell**.

Fernand *masc* a French form of **Ferdinand**.

Fernanda *fem* form of **Ferdnand**.

Fernando *masc* a Spanish form of **Ferdinand**.

Ffion *fem* foxglove (*Welsh*).

Fid *fem* a diminutive form of **Fidelia, Fidelis**.

Fidel *masc* a Spanish form of **Fidelis**.

Fidèle *masc* a French form of **Fidelis**.

Fidelia *fem* a variant form of **Fidelis**; a diminutive form is **Fid**.

Fidelio *masc* an Italian form of **Fidelis**.

Fidelis *masc, fem* faithful (*Latin*); a *fem* variant form is **Fidelia**; a diminutive is **Fid**.

Fidelma *fem* faithful Mary (*Latin/Irish Gaelic*); a diminutive form is **Delma**.

Fielding *masc* a surname, meaning dweller in a field, used as a first name (*Old English*).

Fifi *fem* a French diminutive form of **Josephine**.

Filippo *masc* the Italian form of **Philip**.

Filippa *fem* the Italian form of **Philippa**.

Findlay *masc* a variant form of **Finlay**.

Fingal *masc* white stranger (*Scots Gaelic*).

Finlay, Finley *masc* fair warrior or calf (*Scots Gaelic*); a variant form is **Findlay**.

Finn *masc* fair, white (*Irish Gaelic*); a variant form is **Fionn**.

Finola *fem* a variant form of **Fionnuala**.

Fiona *fem* white, fair (*Scots Gaelic*).

Fionn *masc* a variant form of **Finn**.

Fionnuala *fem* white shoulder (*Irish Gaelic*); a diminutive form is **Nuala**, also used independently.

Fiske *masc* a surname, meaning fish, used as a first name (*Old English*).

Fitch *masc* a surname, meaning point, used as a first name (*Old English*).

Fitz *masc* son (*Old French*); a diminutive form of names beginning with Fitz-.

Fitzgerald *masc* a surname, meaning son of Gerald, used as a first name (*Old French*); a diminutive form is **Fitz**.

Fitzhugh *masc* a surname, meaning son of Hugh, used as a first name (*Old French*); a diminutive form is **Fitz**.

Fitzpatrick *masc* a surname, meaning son of Patrick, used as a first name (*Old French*); a diminutive form is **Fitz**.

Fitzroy *masc* a surname, meaning (illegitimate) son of the king, used as a first name (*Old French*); a diminutive form is **Fitz**.

Flann *masc* red-haired (*Irish Gaelic*).

Flanna *fem* form of **Flann**.

Flannan *masc* red-complexioned (*Irish Gaelic*).

Flavia *fem* yellow-haired, golden (*Latin*).

Flavian, Flavius *masc* forms of Flavia.

Fleming *masc* a surname, meaning man from Flanders, used as a first name (*Old French*).

Fletcher *masc* a surname meaning arrow-maker, used as a first name (*Old French*).

Fleur *fem* a flower (*French*).

Fleurette *fem* little flower (*French*).

Flinn *masc* a variant form of **Flynn**.

Flint *masc* stream, brook (*Old English*).

Flo *fem* a diminutive form of **Flora, Florence**.

Flora *fem* flowers; the Roman goddess of flowers (*Latin*); diminutive forms are **Flo, Florrie, Flossie**.

Florence *fem* blooming; flourishing (*Latin*); diminutive forms are **Flo, Florrie, Flossie, Floy**.

Florian *masc* flowering, blooming (*Latin*).

Florrie, Flossie *fem* diminutive forms of **Flora, Florence**.

Flower *fem* the English word for a bloom or blossom used as a first name.

Floy *fem* a diminutive form of **Flora, Florence**.

Floyd *masc* a variant form of the surname Lloyd used as a first name.

Flynn *masc* a surname, meaning son of the red-haired one, used as a first name (*Scots Gaelic*); a variant form is **Flinn**.

Forbes *masc* a placename and surname, meaning fields or district, used as a first name (*Scots Gaelic*).

Ford *masc* the English word for a crossing place of a river used as a first name (*Old English*).

Forrest, Forrestt *masc* a surname, meaning forest, used as a first name (*Old French*).

Forrester, Forster *masc* a surname, meaning forester, used as a first name (*Old French*).

Fortune *fem* the word for wealth, fate or chance used as a first name (*Latin*); a variant form is **Fortuna**.

Foster *masc* a surname, meaning forester or cutler (*Old French*) or foster parent (*Old English*), used as a first name.

Fra *masc* a diminutive form of **Francis**.

Fraine *masc* a variant form of **Frayn**.

Fran *fem* a diminutive form of **Frances**.

Franca *fem* a diminutive form of **Francesca**.

Frances *fem* form of **Francis**; diminutive forms are **Fanny, Fran, Francie**.

Francesca *fem* the Italian form of **Frances**; a diminutive form is **Francheschina**.

Francesco *masc* the Italian form of **Francis**; a contracted form is **Franco**.

Francie *fem* a diminutive form of **Frances**.

Francine *fem* a diminutive form of **Frances, Françoise**.

Francis *masc* free (*Germanic*); diminutive forms are **Fra, Frank, Francie**.

Francisca *fem* the Spanish form of **Frances**.

Francisco *masc* the Spanish form of **Francis**.

Franco *masc* a contracted form of **Francesco**.

François *masc* the French form of **Francis**.

Françoise *fem* the French form of **Frances**.

Frank *masc* Frenchman (*Old French*) a diminutive
form of **Francis, Franklin**; diminutive forms are
Frankie, Franky.

Franklin, Franklen, Franklyn *masc* a surname,
meaning freeholder, used as a first name (*Old
French*); diminutive forms are **Frank, Frankie,
Franky**.

Frans *masc* the Swedish form of **Francis**.

Franz, Franziskus *masc* German forms of **Francis**.

Franziska *masc* the German form of **Frances**.

Fraser, Frasier *masc* a Scottish surname, meaning
from Frisselle or Fresel in France—possibly straw-
berry, used as a first name (*French*); variant forms are
Frazer, Frazier.

Frayn, Frayne *masc* a surname, meaning ash tree, used
as a surname (*Old French*); a variant form is **Fraine**.

Frazer, Frazier *masc* variant forms of **Fraser**.

Freda *fem* a diminutive form of **Winifred**; a variant
form of **Frieda**.

Frédéric *masc* the French form of **Frederick**.

Frederica *fem* form of Frederick; diminutive forms are
Fred, Freddie, Freddy, Frieda.

Frederick, Frederic *masc* abounding in peace; peaceful ruler (*Germanic*); diminutive forms are **Fred, Freddie, Freddy**.

Frédérique *fem* the French form of **Frederica**.

Fredrik *masc* the Swedish form of **Frederick**.

Freeman *masc* a surname, meaning free man, used as first name (*Old English*).

Frewin *masc* a surname, meaning generous friend, used as a first name (*Old English*).

Freya *fem* lady, the Norse goddess of love (*Norse*).

Frieda *fem* peace (*Germanic*); a diminutive form of **Frederica**.

Friede *fem* the German form of **Frieda**.

Friederike *fem* the German form of **Frederica**; a diminutive form is **Fritzi**.

Friedrich *masc* German forms of **Frederick**; a diminutive form is **Fritz**.

Fritz *masc* a diminutive form of **Friedrich**, also used independently.

Fritzi *fem* a diminutive form of **Friederike**.

Fulton *masc* a surname, meaning muddy place, used as a first name (*Old English*).

Fulvia *fem* yellow-haired (*Latin*).

Fyfe, Fyffe *masc* a surname, meaning from Fife, used as a first name.

G

Gabe *masc* diminutive form of **Gabriel**.

Gabbie, Gabby *fem* diminutive forms of **Gabrielle**.

Gabriel *masc* man of God; in the Bible one of the archangels (*Hebrew*); a diminutive form is **Gabe**.

Gabrielle *fem* form of **Gabriel**; diminutive forms are **Gabbie, Gabby**.

Gaea *fem* the Latin form of **Gaia**.

Gaia *fem* earth, in classical mythology the goddess of the earth (*Greek*); the Latin form is **Gaea**.

Gail *fem* a diminutive form of **Abigail**, now used independently; variant forms are **Gale, Gayle**.

Galatea *fem* white as milk, in Greek mythology a statue brought to life (*Greek*)

Gale *fem* a variant form of **Gail**; *masc* a surname, meaning jail, used as a first name (*Old French*).

Galen *masc* the anglicized form of the Roman family name *Galenus*, calmer (*Latin*).

Galia *fem* wave (*Hebrew*).

Gallagher *masc* a surname, meaning foreign helper, used as a first name (*Irish Gaelic*).

Galloway *masc* a placename and surname, meaning stranger, used as a first name (*Scots Gaelic*)

Galton *masc* a surname, meaning rented farm, used as a first name (*Old English*).

Galvin *masc* bright, white (*Irish Gaelic*).

Gamaliel *masc* reward of God (Hebr*ew*).

Gardenia *fem* the name of a flowering plant with fragrant flowers, called after Dr Alexander Garden, used as a first name (*New Latin*).

Gareth *masc* old man (*Welsh*); diminutive forms are **Gary, Garry**; a variant form is **Garth**.

Garfield *masc* a surname, meaning triangular piece of open land, used as a first name (*Old English*).

Garland *fem* the name for a wreath or crown of flowers used as a first name (*Old French*); *masc* a surname, meaning a maker of metal garlands, used as a first name (*Old English*).

Garnet *fem* the name of a deep-red gemstone used as a first name (*Old French*).

Garnet, Garnett *masc* a surname, meaning pomegranate, used as a first name (*Old French*).

Garret, Garrett *masc* the Irish Gaelic form of **Gerard**; a variant form of **Garrard**.

Garrard *masc* a variant form of **Gerard**.

Garrison *masc* a surname, meaning son of Garret, used as a first name (*Old English*).

Garry *masc* a variant form of **Gary**; a placename,

meaning rough water, used as a first name (*Scots Gaelic*).

Garth *masc* a surname, meaning garden or paddock, used as a first name (*Old Norse*); a variant form of **Gareth**.

Garton *masc* a surname, meaning fenced farm, used as a first name (*Old Norse*).

Garve *masc* a placename, meaning rough place, used as a first name (*Scots Gaelic*).

Gary *masc* spear carrier (*Germanic*); a diminutive form of **Gareth**; a variant form is **Garry**.

Gaspard *masc* the French form of **Jasper**.

Gaston *masc* stranger, guest (*Germanic*); from Gascony (*Old French*).

Gautier, Gauthier *masc* French forms of **Walter**.

Gavin *masc* an anglicized form of **Gawain**.

Gawain *masc* white hawk (*Welsh*).

Gay *fem* an English adjective, meaning being joyous used as a first name (*Old French*); *masc* an Irish diminutive form of **Gabriel**.

Gayle *fem* a variant form of **Gail**.

Gaylord *masc* a surname, meaning brisk noble man, used as a first name (*Old French*).

Gaynor *fem* a medieval English form of **Guinevere**.

Gazella *fem* like a gazelle or antelope (*Latin*).

Gemma *fem* the Italian word for a gem used as a first name; a variant form is **Jemma**.

Gene *masc* a diminutive form of **Eugene**, now used independently.

Geneva *fem* a variant form of **Genevieve**; the name of a Swiss city used as a first name.

Genevieve *fem* meaning uncertain, possibly tribe woman (*Celtic*).

Geneviève *fem* the French form of **Genevieve**.

Geoffrey *masc* a variant form of **Jeffrey**; a diminutive form is **Geoff**.

Georg *masc* the German form of **George**.

George *masc* a landholder; husbandman (*Germanic*); diminutive forms are **Geordie, Georgie, Georgy**.

Georges *masc* the French form of **George**.

Georgia, Georgiana, Georgina *fem* forms of **George**; a diminutive form is **Georgie**.

Geraint *masc* old man (*Welsh*).

Gerald *masc* strong with the spear (*Germanic*); diminutive forms are **Gerrie, Gerry, Jerry**.

Geraldine *fem* form of **Gerald**.

Gerard *masc* firm spear (*Old German*); variant forms are **Garrard, Garratt, Gerrard**; diminutive forms are **Gerrie, Gerry, Jerry**.

Gérard *masc* the French form of **Gerard**.

Gerardo *masc* the Italian form of **Gerard**.

Géraud *masc* a French form of **Gerald**.

Gerhard *masc* the German form of **Gerard**.

Gerhold *masc* a German form of **Gerald**.

Germain *masc* brother (*Latin*); diminutive forms are
   Gerrie, Gerry.

Germaine *fem* form of **Germain**; a variant form is
   Jermaine.

Geronimo, Gerolamo *masc* Italian forms of **Jerome**.

Gerrie, Gerry *masc* diminutive forms of **Gerald,
   Gerard**; *fem* a diminutive form of **Geraldine**.

Gershom *masc* a stranger there (*Hebrew*).

Gertrude *fem* spear maiden (*Germanic*); diminutive
   forms are **Gert, Gertie, Trudi, Trudy**.

Gervas *masc* the German form of **Gervase**.

Gervase, Gervaise *masc* spearman (*Germanic*); variant
   forms are **Gervaise, Jarvis, Jervis**.

Gervais *masc* the French form of **Gervase**.

Gervaise *masc* a variant form of **Gervase**.

Gervasio *masc* the Italian, Portuguese and Spanish
   form of **Gervase**.

Gethin *masc* dusky (*Welsh*).

Giacomo *masc* an Italian form of **James**.

Gian, Gianni *masc* diminutive forms of **Giovanni**.

Gibson *masc* a surname, meaning son of Gilbert, used
   as a first name (*Old English*).

Gideon *masc* of a hill (*Hebrew*).

Giffard, Gifford *masc* a surname, meaning bloated
   (*Old French*) or gift (*Germanic*).

Gigi *fem* a French diminutive form of **Georgine,
   Virginie**.

Gil *masc* a diminutive form of **Gilbert, Gilchrist, Giles**; a Spanish form of **Giles**.

Gilbert *masc* yellow-bright; famous (*Germanic*); diminutive form is **Gil**.

Gilberta, Gilberte *fem* forms of **Gilbert**; diminutive forms are **Gill, Gillie, Gilly**.

Gilchrist *masc* servant of Christ (*Scots Gaelic*); a diminutive form is **Gil**.

Gilda *fem* sacrifice (*Germanic*).

Giles *masc* a kid (*Greek*); a diminutive form is **Gil**.

Gill *fem* a diminutive form of **Gilberta, Gilberte, Gillian**.

Gilles *masc* the French form of **Giles**.

Gillespie *masc* a surname, meaning servant of a bishop, used as a first name (*Scots Gaelic*).

Gillie *fem* a diminutive form of **Gilberta, Gilberte, Gillian**.

Gillian *fem* form of **Julian**; diminutive forms are **Gill, Gillie, Gilly**.

Gillmore *masc* a variant form of **Gilmore**.

Gilly *fem* a diminutive form of **Gilberta, Gilberte, Gillian**.

Gilmore, Gilmour *masc* a surname, meaning servant of St Mary, used as a first name (*Scots Gaelic*); a variant form is **Gillmore**.

Gilroy *masc* a surname, meaning servant of the red haired one, used as a first name (*Gaelic*).

Gina *fem* a diminutive form of **Georgina**, also used
   independently.

Ginnie, Ginny *fem* a diminutive form of **Virginia**.

Gioacchino *masc* the Italian form of **Joachim**.

Giorgio *masc* the Italian form of **George**.

Giovanna *fem* the Italian form of **Jane**.

Giovanni *masc* the Italian form of **John**; diminutive
   forms are **Gian, Gianni**.

Gipsy *fem* a variant form of **Gypsy**.

Giraldo *masc* the Italian form of **Gerald**.

Giraud, Girauld *masc* French forms of **Gerald**.

Girolamo *masc* an Italian form of **Jerome**.

Girvan *masc* a placename, meaning short river, used as
   a first name (*Scots Gaelic*).

Giselle *fem* promise, pledge (*Germanic*)

Gisela *fem* the Dutch and German form of **Giselle**.

Gisèle *fem* the French form of **Giselle**.

Gitana *fem* gipsy (*Spanish*).

Giulio *masc* the Italian form of **Julius**.

Giuseppe *masc* the Italian form of **Joseph**; a diminutive form is **Beppe, Beppo**.

Gladwin *masc* a surname, meaning glad friend, used as
   a first name (*Old English*).

Gladys *fem* the anglicized Welsh form of **Claudia**.

Glanville *masc* Dweller on the oak tree estate (*French*);
   a diminutive form is **Glanvil**.

Gleda *fem* Old English version of Gladys (*Old English*).

Glen *masc* the surname, meaning a valley, used as a
first name (*Scots Gaelic*); a variant form is **Glenn**.

Glenda *fem* clean and good (*Welsh*); a variant form is
Glenys.

Glendon *masc* From the fortress in the Glen (*Celtic*).

Glenn *masc* a variant form of **Glen**, now also used as a
feminine name.

Glenna *fem* form of **Glen**.

Glenys *fem* a variant form of **Glenda**; a variant form is
Glynis.

Gloria *fem* glory (*Latin*).

Glyn *masc* valley (*Welsh*); a variant form is **Glynn**.

Glynis *fem* form of **Glyn**; a variant form of **Glenys**.

Glynn *masc* a variant form of **Glyn**.

Goddard *masc* God strong (*Old German*).

Godfrey *masc* God peace (*Germanic*).

Godiva *fem* God gift (*Old English*)**u**.

Godwin *masc* God friend (*Old English*).

Golda, Golde *fem* gold (*Yiddish*).

Goldie *fem* an anglized form of **Golda**; fair-haired
(*English*).

Golding *masc* a surname, meaning son of gold, used as
a first name (*Old English*).

Goldwin *masc* gold friend (*Old English*).

Goodwin *masc* a surname, meaning good friend, used
as a first name; (*Old English*).

Gordon *masc* a surname, meaning great hill, used as a

first name (*Scots Gaelic*).

Gottfried *masc* the German form of **Godfrey**; a diminutive form is **Götz**.

Grace *fem* grace (*Latin*); a diminutive form is **Gracie**.

Grady *masc* a surname, meaning noble, used as a first name (*Irish Gaelic*).

Graham, Grahame, Graeme *masc* a Scottish surname, meaning gravelly homestead, used as a first name (*Old English*).

Gráinne *fem* love (*Irish Gaelic*).

Granger *masc* a surname, meaning farmer or bailiff, used as a first name (*Old English*).

Grant *masc* a surname, meaning large, used as a first name (*Norman French*).

Granville *masc* large town (*Old French*).

Gray *masc* a surname, meaning grey-haired, used as a first name (*Old English*); a variant form is **Grey**.

Greeley *masc* a surname, meaning pitted, used as a first name (*Old English*).

Greer *fem* form of the surname **Grier**.

Grégoire *masc* the French form of **Gregory**.

Gregor *masc* a Scots form of **Gregory**.

Gregorio *masc* the Italian and Spanish form of **Gregory**.

Gregory *masc* watchman (*Greek*); a diminutive form is **Greg**.

Gresham *masc* a surname, meaning grazing meadow,

used as a first name (*Old English*).

Greta *fem* a diminutive form of **Margaret**.

Gretchen *fem* a diminutive form of **Margaret, Margarete**.

Grete *fem* a diminutive form of **Margarete**.

Greville *masc* a surname, meaning from Gréville in France, used as a first name.

Grier *masc*, *fem* a surname, a contracted form of **Gregor**, used as a first name; a variant *fem* form is **Greer**.

Griff *masc* a diminutive form of **Griffin, Griffith**.

Griffin *masc* a Latinized form of **Griffith**; a diminutive form is **Griff**.

Griffith *masc* an anglicized form of **Gruffydd**; a diminutive form is **Griff**.

Griselda, Grizelda *fem* stone heroine (*Germanic*); diminutive forms are **Grissel, Grizel, Grizzel**.

Grover *masc* a surname, meaning from a grove of trees, used as a first name (*Old English*).

Gruffydd *masc* powerful chief (*Welsh*).

Gualterio *masc* the Spanish form of **Walter**.

Gualtieri *masc* the Italian form of **Walter**.

Gudrun *fem* war spell, rune (*Old Norse*)a.

Guglielmo *masc* the Italian form of **William**.

Guido *masc* the German, Italian, and Spanish forms of **Guy**.

Guilbert *masc* a French form of **Gilbert**.

Guillaume *masc* the French form of **William**.

Guillermo, Guillelmo *masc* Spanish forms of **William**.

Guinevere *fem* white and soft, the name of the wife of King Arthur (*Welsh*).

Gunhilda, Gunhilde *fem* stife war (*Old Norse*).

Gunnar *masc* the Scandinavian form of **Gunter**.

Gunter *masc* battle warrior (*Germanic*).

Günther *masc* the German form of **Gunter**.

Gus *masc* a diminutive form of **Angus, Augustus, Gustave**.

Gussie, Gusta *fem* diminutive forms of **Augusta**.

Gustaf *masc* the Swedish form of **Gustave**.

Gustave, Gustavus *masc* staff of the Goths (*Swedish*); a diminutive form is **Gus**.

Guthrie *masc* a surname, meaning windy, used as a first name (*Scots Gaelic*).

Guy *masc* a leader (*German-French*).

Guyon *masc* a French form of **Guy**.

Gwenda *fem* a diminutive form of **Gwendolen**, also used independently.

Gwendolen, Gwendolin, Gwendolyn *fem* white ring or bow (*Welsh*); diminutive forms are **Gwen, Gwenda, Gwennie**.

Gwillym, Gwilym *masc* Welsh forms of **William**.

Gwyneth, Gwynneth *fem* blessed (*Welsh*).

Gwyn, Gwynn *masc* fair, blessed (*Welsh*); diminutive forms are **Gwyn, Guin**.

Gwynfor *masc* fair lord (*Welsh*).

Gypsy *fem* the name for a member of a people who live a nomadic life used as a first name; a variant form is **Gipsy**.

H

Haakon *masc* a variant form of **Hakon**.

Hackett *masc* a surname, meaning little woodcutter, used as a first name (*Old Norse*).

Haddan, Hadden, Haddon *masc* a surname, meaning heathery hill, used as a first name (*Old English*).

Hadley *masc* a surname, meaning heathery hill or heathery meadow, used as a first name (*Old English*).

Hadrian *masc* a variant form of **Adrian**.

Hagar *fem* flight (*Hebrew*).

Hagan, Hagan *masc* young Hugh (*Irish Gaelic*); thorn bush or thorn fence (*Germanic*).

Hagley *masc* a surname, meaning haw wood or clearing, used as a first name (*Old English*).

Haidee *fem* modest, honoured (*Greek*); a variant form of **Heidi**.

Haig *masc* a first name, meaning one who lives in an enclosure, used as a first name (*Old English*).

Hakon *masc* from the exalted race (*Old Norse*); a variant form is **Haakon**; a diminutive form is **Hako**.

Hal *masc* a diminutive form of **Halbert, Henry**.

Halbert *masc* brilliant hero (*Old English*); a diminutive
form is **Hal**.

Halcyon, Halcyone *fem* variant forms of **Alcyone**.

Haldan, Haldane, Halden, Haldin *fem* a surname,
meaning half Dane, used as a surname (*Old English*).

Hale *masc* a surname, meaning from the hall, used as a
surname (*Old English*).

Haley *masc, fem* a variant form of **Hayley**.

Halford *masc* a surname, meaning from a ford in a
hollow, used as a first name (*Old English*).

Haliwell *masc* a variant form of **Halliwell**.

Hall *masc* a surname, meaning one who lives at a
manor house, used as a first name (*Old English*).

Hallam *masc* a surname, meaning at the hollow (*Old
English*), or a placename, meaning at the rocky place
(*Old Norse*), used as a first name.

Halliwell *masc* a surname, meaning one who lives by
the holy well, used as a first name (*Old English*); a
variant form is **Haliwell**.

Halstead, Halsted *masc* a surname, meaning from the
stronghold, used as a first name (*Old English*).

Halton *masc* a surname, meaning from the lookout hill,
used as a first name (*Old English*).

Hamar *masc* strong man (*Old Norse*).

Hamilton *masc* a surname, meaning farm in broken
country, used as a first name. (*Old English*).

Hamish *masc* a Scots Gaelic form of **James**.

Hamlet, Hamlett *masc* a surname, meaning little
   home, used as a first name (*Germanic*).

Hammond *masc* a surname, meaning belonging to
   Hamon, used as a first name (*Old English*).

Hamon *masc* great protection (*Old English*).

Hanford *masc* a surname, meaning rocky ford or ford
   with cocks, used as a first name (*Old English*).

Hank *masc* a diminutive form of **Henry**.

Hanley *masc* a surname, meaning from the high
   meadow or hill, used as a first name (*Old English*).

Hannah *fem* grace (*Hebrew*); a variant form is **Ann**; a
   diminutive form is **Nana**.

Hannibal *masc* grace of Baal (*Punic*).

Hans *masc* a diminutive form of **Johann**.

Hansel *masc* gift from God (*Scandinavian*).

Happy *fem* an English adjective, meaning feeling,
   showing or expressing joy, now used as a first name
   (*Old English*).

Haralda *fem* form of **Harold**.

Harbert *masc* a variant form of **Herbert**.

Harcourt *masc* a surname, meaning from a fortified
   court (*Old French*), or falconer's cottage (*Old
   English*), used as a first name.

Harden *masc* a surname, meaning the valley of the
   hare, used as a first name (*Old English*).

Hardie, Hardey *masc* variant forms of **Hardy**.

Harding *masc* a surname, meaning brave warrior, used

as a first name (*Old English*).

Hardy *masc* a surname, meaning bold and daring, used
as a first name (*Germanic*); variant forms are
Hardey, Hardie.

Harford *masc* a surname, meaning stags' ford, used as
a first name (*Old English*).

Hargrave, Hargreave, Hargreaves *masc* a surname,
meaning from the hare grove, used as a first name
(*Old English*).

Harlan, Harland *masc* a surname, meaning rocky land,
used as a first name (*Old English*).

Harley *masc* a surname, meaning from the hare
meadow or hill, used as a first name (*Old English*).

Harlow *masc* a placename and surname, meaning
fortified hill, used as a first name (*Old English*).

Harmony *fem* the word for the quality of concord used
as a first name (*Greek*).

Harold *masc* a champion; general of an army (*Old
English*).

Harper *masc* a surname, meaning harp player or
maker, used as a first name (*Old English*).

Harriet, Harriot *fem* forms of **Harry**; diminutive
forms are **Hattie, Hatty**.

Harris, Harrison *masc* surnames, meaning son of
Harold or Harry, used as a first name (*Old English*)

Harry *masc* a diminutive form of **Henry**, also used
independently.

Hart *masc* a surname, meaning hart deer, used as a first name (*Old English*).

Hartford *masc* a placename and surname, meaning ford of the deer, or army ford, used as a first name (*Old English*); a variant form is **Hertford**.

Hartley *masc* a surname, meaning clearing with stags, used as a first name (*Old English*).

Hartmann, Hartman *masc* strong and brave (*Germanic*).

Hartwell *masc* a surname, meaning stags' stream, used as a first name (*Old English*).

Harvey, Harvie *masc* a surname, meaning battle worthy, used as a first name (*Breton Gaelic*); a variant form is **Hervey**.

Haslett, Hazlitt *masc* variant forms of **Hazlett**.

Hastings *masc* a placename and surname, meaning territory of the violent ones, used as a first name (*Old English*).

Hattie, Hatty *fem* a diminutive form of **Harriet**.

Havelock *masc* a surname, meaning sea battle, used as a first name (*Old Norse*).

Hawley *masc* a surname, meaning from a hedged meadow, used as a first name (*Old English*).

Hayden, Haydon *masc* a surname, meaning heather hill or hay hill, used as a first name (*Old English*).

Hayley *masc, fem* a surname, meaning hay clearing, used as a first name (*Old English*); a variant form is **Haley**.

Hayward *masc* a surname, meaning supervisor of
enclosures, used as a first name (*Old English*); a
variant form is **Heyward**.

Haywood *masc* a surname, meaning fenced forest, used
as a first name (*Old English*); a variant form is
Heywood.

Hazel *fem* the name of a tree used as a first name (*Old
English*).

Hazlett, Hazlitt *masc* a surname, meaning hazel tree,
used as a first name (*Old English*); variant forms are
Haslett, Hazlitt.

Heath *masc* a surname, meaning heathland, used as a
first name (*Old English*).

Heathcliff, Heathcliffe *masc* dweller by the heather
cliff (*Old English*).

Heather *fem* the name of a purple or white-flowered
plant of the heath family used as a first name.

Hebe *fem* young (*Greek*). In Greek mythology, the
daughter of Zeus and goddess of youth and spring.

Hector *masc* holding fast (*Greek*).

Hedda *fem* war, strife (*Germanic*).

Hedwig, Hedvig *fem* strife (*Germanic*).

Hefin *masc* summery (*Welsh*).

Heidi *fem* diminutive of **Adelheid**; a variant form is
Haidee.

Heinrich *masc* the German form of **Henry**; diminutive
forms are **Heinz, Heinze**.

Helen, Helena *fem* light (*Greek*); diminutive forms are
  Nell, Lena.

Helene *fem* the German form of **Helen**.

Hélène *fem* the French form of **Helen**.

Helga *fem* healthy, happy, holy (*Old Norse*).

Helge *masc* form of **Helga**.

Helma *fem* protection (*Germanic*).

Héloïse *fem* a French variant form of **Éloise**.

Hendrik *masc* the Dutch form of **Henry**.

Henri *masc* the French form of **Henry**.

Henrietta *fem* form of **Henry**; diminutive forms are
  Hettie, Hetty, Netta, Nettie.

Henriette *fem* the French form of **Henrietta**.

Henry *masc* the head or chief of a house (*Germanic*);
  diminutive forms are **Harry, Hal, Hank**.

Hephzibah *fem* my delight is in her (*Hebrew*); a
  diminutive form is **Hepsy**.

Hera *fem* queen of heaven; in Greek mythology, the
  sister and wife of Zeus (*Greek*). Her counterpart in
  Roman mythology is Juno.

Herakles *masc* the Greek counterpart of **Hercules**.

Herbert *masc* army bright (*Old English*); a variant
  form is **Harbert**; diminutive forms are **Herb,
  Herbie**.

Hercule *masc* the French form of **Hercules**.

Hercules *masc* glory of Hera (the Latin form of the
  name of Herakles, the Greek hero, son of Zeus and

stepson of Hera).

Heribert *masc* the German form of **Herbert**.

Herman *masc* warrior (*Germanic*).

Hermann *masc* the German form of **Herman**.

Hermes *masc* in Greek mythology, the messenger of the gods, with winged feet. His counterpart in Roman mythology is Mercury.

Hermione *fem* a name derived from that of **Hermes**.

Hermosa *fem* beautiful (*Spanish*).

Hernando *masc* a Spanish form of **Ferdinand**.

Herrick *masc* a surname, meaning powerful army, used as a first name (*Old Norse*).

Herta *fem* of the earth (*Old English*); a variant form is **Hertha**.

Hertford *masc* a variant form of **Hartford**.

Hertha *fem* a variant form of **Herta**.

Hervé *masc* a French form of **Harvey**.

Hervey *masc* a variant form of **Harvey**.

Hesketh *masc* a surname, meaning horse track, used as a first name (*Old Norse*).

Hester, Hesther *fem* variant forms of **Esther**.

Hettie, Hetty *fem* diminutive forms of **Henrietta**.

Heulwen *fem* sunshine (*Welsh*).

Hew *masc* a Welsh form of **Hugh**.

Hewett, Hewit *masc* a surname, meaning little Hugh or cleared place, used as a first name (*Old English*).

Heyward *masc* a variant form of **Hayward**.

Heywood *masc* a variant form of **Haywood**.

Hezekiah *masc* strength of the Lord (*Hebrew*).

Hi *masc* a diminutive form of **Hiram, Hyram**.

Hibernia *fem* the Latin name for Ireland used as a first name.

Hibiscus *fem* marsh mallow, the name of a brightly flowering plant used as a first name (*Greek/Latin*).

Hieronymus *masc* the Latin and German forms of **Jerome**.

Hilaire *masc* the French form of **Hilary**.

Hilario *masc* the Spanish form of **Hilary**.

Hilary, Hillary *masc fem* cheerful; merry (*Latin*).

Hilda *fem* battle maid (*Germanic*); a variant form is **Hylda**.

Hildebrand *masc* battle sword (*Germanic*).

Hildegarde *fem* strong in battle (*Germanic*).

Hilton *masc* a surname, meaning from the hill farm, used as a first name (*Old English*); a variant form is **Hylton**.

Hiram *masc* brother of the exalted one (*Hebrew*); a variant form is **Hyram**; a diminutive form is **Hi**.

Hobart *masc* a variant form of **Hubert**.

Hogan *masc* youthful (*Irish Gaelic*).

Holbert, Holbird *masc* variant forms of **Hulbert**.

Holbrook *masc* a surname, meaning brook in the valley, used as a first name (*Old English*).

Holcomb, Holcombe *masc* a surname, meaning deep valley, used as a first name (*Old English*).

Holden *masc* a surname, meaning from the deep valley, used as a first name (*Old English*).

Holgate *masc* a surname, meaning road in a hollow, used as a first name (*Old English*).

Hollis *masc* a surname, meaning dweller near holly trees, used as a first name (*Old English*).

Holly, Hollie *fem* the name of the red-berried tree used as a first name (*English*).

Holmes *masc* a surname, meaning an island in a river, used as a first name (*Old English*).

Holt *masc* a surname, meaning a wood or forest, used as a first name (*Old English*).

Homer *masc* uncertain, possibly hostage (*Greek*); the name of the Greek epic poet of the first milennium BC.

Honey *fem* the word for a sweet substance used as a term of endearment and as a first name.

Honor, Honora *fem* variant forms of **Honour**.

Honoria *fem* honourable (*Latin*); diminutive forms are **Nora, Norah, Noreen**.

Honorius *masc* form of **Honoria**.

Honour *fem* the word for personal intregity used as a first name; variant forms are **Honor, Honora**.

Hope *fem* the word for the feeling of expectation used as a first name (*English*).

Horace, Horatio *masc* origin uncertain, possibly a family name *Horatius* (*Latin*).

Horatia *fem* form of **Horace**.

Hortensia, Hortense *fem* of the garden (*Latin*).

Horton *masc* a surname, meaning muddy place, used as a first name (*Old English*).

Hosea *masc* salvation (*Hebrew*).

Houghton *masc* a surname, meaning place in an enclosure, used as a first name (*Old English*); a variant form is **Hutton**.

Houston, Houstun *masc* a surname, meaning Hugh's place, used as a first name (*Old English*).

Howard *masc* a surname, meaning mind strong, used as a first name (*Germanic*).

Howe *masc* a surname, meaning high one (*Germanic*) or hill (*Old English*) used as a first name.

Howel, Howell *masc* anglicized forms of **Hywel**.

Hubert *masc* mind bright (*Germanic*); a variant surname form is **Hobart**.

Huberta *fem* form of **Hubert**.

Hudson *masc* a surname, meaning son of little Hugh, used as a first name (*Old English*).

Hugh *masc* mind; spirit; soul (*Danish*).

Hugo *masc* the Latin, German, and Spanish form of **Hugh**.

Hugues *masc* the French form of **Hugh**.

Hulbert, Hulburd, Hulburt *masc* a surname, meaning brilliant, gracious, used as a first name (*Germanic*); variant forms are **Holbert, Holbird**.

Hulda, Huldah *fem* weasel (*Hebrew*).

Humbert *masc* bright warrior (*Germanic*).

Humphrey, Humphry *masc* giant peace (*Old English*); diminutive forms are **Hump, Humph**.

Hunt, Hunter *masc* surnames, meaning hunter, used as first names (*Old English*).

Huntingdon *masc* a placename and surname, meaning hunter's hill, used as a first name (*Old English*).

Huntington *masc* a surname, meaning hunter's farm, used as a first name (*Old English*).

Huntley, Huntly *masc* a surname, meaning hunter's meadow, used as a first name (*Old English*).

Hurley *masc* sea tide (*Gaelic*).

Hurst *masc* a surname, meaning wooded hill, used as a first name (*Old English*).

Hutton *masc* a variant form of **Houghton**.

Huw *masc* a Welsh variant form of **Hugh**.

Huxley *masc* a surname, meaning Hugh's meadow, used as a first name (*Old English*).

Hyacinth *fem* the name of the flower adapted from the name of the hero of Greek mythology whose blood after his killing by Apollo caused a flower to spring up.

Hyam *masc* man of life (*Hebrew*); a variant form is **Hyman**; diminutive forms are **Hi, Hy**.

Hyde *masc* a surname, meaning a hide (a measurement unit) of land, used as a first name (*Old English*).

Hylda *fem* a variant form of **Hilda**.

Hylton *masc* a variant form of **Hilton**.

Hyman *masc* a variant form of **Hyam**.

Hypatia *fem* highest (*Greek*).

Hyram *masc* a variant form of **Hiram**; diminutive forms are **Hi, Hy**.

Hywel, Hywell *masc* sound; whole (*Welsh*); anglicized forms are **Howel, Howell**.

I

Iachimo *masc* an Italian form of **James**.

Iacovo *masc* an Italian form of **Jacob**.

Ian *masc* an anglicized form of **Iain**.

Iain *masc* the Scots Gaelic form of **John**.

Ianthe *fem* violet flower (*Greek*).

Ibby *fem* a diminutive form of **Isabel**.

Ichabod *masc* inglorious (*Hebrew*).

Ida *fem* god-like (*Germanic*).

Idabell *fem* god-like and fair.

Idris *masc* fiery lord (*Welsh*).

Idonia *fem* sufficient (*Latin*).

Idony, Idonie *fem* in Norse mythology, the keeper of the golden apples of youth (*Norse*).

Iestyn *masc* the Welsh form of **Justin**.

Ieuan, Ifan *masc* Welsh forms of **John**; a variant form is **Iwan**.

Ifor *masc* a Welsh form of **Ivor**.

Ignace *masc* the French form of **Ignatius**.

Ignacio *masc* a Spanish form of **Ignatius**.

Ignatia *fem* form of **Ignatius**.

Ignatius *masc* from *ignis*, fire (*Greek*).

Ignatz, Ignaz *masc* German forms of **Ignatius**.

Ignazio *masc* the Italian form of **Ignatius**.

Igor *masc* the Russian form of **Ivor**.

Ike *masc* a diminutive form of **Isaac**.

Ilario *masc* the Italian form of **Hilary**.

Ilona *fem* a Hungarian form of **Helen**; a diminutive
    form is **Ilka**.

Ilse *fem* a diminutive form of **Elisabeth**.

Immanuel *masc* a variant form of Emmanuel; a
    diminutive form is **Manny**.

Imogen *fem* from *innogen*, girl, maiden (*Celtic*), used
    by Shakespeare for one of his characters in
    Cymbeline and misspelled by him or his printer.

Imperial *fem* relating to an emperor (*Latin*).

Imre *masc* a Hungarian form of **Emeric**.

Ina *fem* a diminutive form of names ending in *-ina*, e.g.
    Georgina, Wilhelmina.

Inés, Inez *fem* Spanish forms of **Agnes**.

Inga *fem* a diminutive form of **Ingeborg, Ingrid**.

Inge *masc* a diminutive form of **Ingemar**; *fem* a
    diminutive form of **Ingeborg, Ingrid**.

Ingeborg *fem* fortification of Ing, the god of fertility
    (Frey) (*Old Norse*); diminutive forms are **Inga, Inge**.

Ingemar *masc* famous son of Ing (*Old Norse*); a variant
    form is **Ingmar**; a diminutive form is **Inge**.

Inger *fem* a variant form of **Ingrid**.

Ingmar *masc* a variant form of **Ingemar**.

Ingram *masc* a surname, meaning raven angel (*Germanic*) or river meadow (*Old English*), used as a first name.

Ingrid *fem* maiden of Ing, the god of fertility (Frey) (*Old Norse*); a variant form is **Inger**; diminutive forms are **Inga, Inge**.

Inigo *masc* a Spanish form of **Ignatius**, now used as an English-language form.

Innes, Inness *masc, fem* a surname, meaning island, used as a first name (*Scots Gaelic*).

Iola *fem* a variant form of **Iole**.

Iolanthe *fem* violet flower (*Greek*).

Iole *fem* violet (*Greek*); a variant form is **Iola**.

Iolo, Iolyn *masc* diminutive forms of **Iorwerth**.

Iona *fem* yew tree (*Celtic*), the name of the Scottish Hebridean island used as a first name.

Ione*fem* a violet (*Greek*)

Iorwerth *masc* handsome nobleman (*Welsh*); diminutive forms are **Iolo, Iolyn**.

Iphigenia *fem* strong (*Greek*).

Ira *masc* watchful (*Hebrew*).

Irene *fem* peace (*Greek*); a diminutive form is **Renie**.

Iris *fem* rainbow (*Greek*).

Irma *fem* noble one (Germanic).

Irvine, Irving *masc* a surname, meaning fresh or green river, used as a first name (*Celtic*).

Irwin *masc* a surname, meaning friend of boars, used as a first name (*Old English*).

Isa *fem* a diminutive form of **Isabel**.

Isaac *masc* laughter (*Hebrew*); a variant form is **Izaak**; a diminutive form is **Ike**.

Isabel, Isabella *fem* Spanish forms of **Elizabeth**, now used as separate English-language names; a variant form is **Isobel**; diminutive forms are **Ibby, Isa, Izzie, Izzy, Tib, Tibbie**.

Isabelle *fem* the French form of **Isabel**.

Isadora *fem* a variant form of **Isidora**.

Isaiah *masc* salvation of Jehovah(*Hebrew*).

Iseabail, Ishbel *fem* Scots forms of **Isabel**.

Iseult *fem* a French and Welsh form of **Isolde**.

Isham *masc* a surname, meaning home on the water, used as a first name (*Old English*).

Isidor *masc* the German form of **Isidore**.

Isidora *fem* form of **Isidore**; a variant form is **Isadora**.

Isidore *masc* gift of Isis (*Greek*).

Isidoro *masc* an Italian form of **Isidore**.

Isidro *masc* Spanish forms of **Isidore**.

Isla, Islay *fem* a Scottish island name used as a first name.

Isobel *fem* a variant form of **Isabel**.

Isola *fem* isolated, alone (*Latin*).

Isolde, Isolda, Isold *fem* beautiful aspect (*Welsh*).

Israel *masc* a soldier of God ruling with the Lord

(*Hebrew*); a diminutive form is **Izzy**.

Istvan *masc* the Hungarian form of Stephen.

Ita, Ite *fem* thirst (for truth) (*Irish Gaelic*).

Ivan *masc* the Russian form of **John**.

Ivana *fem* form of **Ivan**.

Ives *masc* a surname, meaning son of Ive (yew), used as a first name (*Germanic*).

Ivo *masc* the Welsh form of **Yves**.

Ivor *masc* yew army (*Old Norse*).

Ivy *masc fem* the name of the plant used as a first name (*English*).

Iwan *masc* a variant form of **Ieuan**.

Izaak *masc* a variant form of **Isaac**.

Izzie, Izzy *masc fem* diminutive forms of **Isabel, Israel**.

J

Jabal *masc* guide (*Hebrew*).

Jabez *masc* causing pain (*Hebrew*).

Jacinta *fem* the Spanish form of **Hyacinth**.

Jacinth *fem* a variant form of **Hyacinth**.

Jack *masc* a diminutive form of **John**, now used independently; diminutive forms are **Jackie, Jacky**.

Jackie, Jacky *masc* a diminutive form of **Jack, John**; *fem* a diminutive form of **Jacqueline**.

Jackson *masc* a surname, meaning son of Jack, used as a first name.

Jacob *masc* supplanter (*Hebrew*); a diminutive form is **Jake**.

Jacoba *fem* fem form of **Jacob**.

Jacobo *masc* the Spanish form of **Jacob**.

Jacqueline *fem* a diminutive form of **Jacques**; a variant form is **Jaqueline**; a diminutive form is **Jackie**.

Jacques *masc* the French form of **Jacob, James**.

Jacquetta *fem* form of **James**.

Jade *fem* the name of the light-green semi-precious stone used as a first name.

Jael *fem* wid she-goat (*Hebrew*).

Jagger *masc* a surname, meaning a carter, used as a first name (*Middle English*).

Jago *masc* a Cornish form of **James**.

Jaime *masc* a Spanish form of **James**; *fem* a variant form of **Jamie**.

Jairus *masc* he will enlighten (*Hebrew*).

Jake *masc* a diminutive form of **Jacob**, now used independently.

Jakob *masc* the German form of **Jacob, James**.

Jamal *masc fem* beauty (*Arabic*).

James *masc* a Christian form of **Jacob**; diminutive forms are **Jamie, Jem, Jim, Jimmy**.

Jamesina *fem* form of **James**; a diminutive form is **Ina**.

Jamie *masc* a diminutive form of **James**, now used independently, often as a girl's name.

Jan *masc* a diminutive form of **John**; the Dutch form of **John**; *fem* a diminutive form of **Jancis, Jane, Janet**, now used independently.

Jancis *fem* a combination of **Jan** and **Frances**; a diminutive form is **Jan**.

Jane *fem* form of **John**; variant forms are **Janet, Janeta, Janette, Janice, Janine, Jayne, Jean, Joan**; diminutive forms are **Jan, Janey, Janie**.

Janet, Janeta, Janette *fem* variant forms of **Jane**; a diminutive form is **Jan**.

Janice *fem* a variant form of **Jane**.

Janine *fem* a variant form of **Janey**.

Japheth *masc* extension (*Hebrew*).

Jaqueline *fem* a variant form of **Jacqueline**; a diminutive form is **Jaqui**.

Jared *masc* (servant (*Hebrew*).

Jarvis *masc* a surname form of **Gervase** used as a first name; a variant form is **Jervis**.

Jasmine, Jamsin *fem* the name of the flower used as a first name; variant forms are **Jessamine, Jessamyn, Yasmin, Yasmine**.

Jason *masc* healer (*Greek*); in Greek mythology, the hero who led the Argonauts.

Jasper *masc* treasure master (*Persian*).

Javan *masc* clay (*Hebrew*).

Javier *masc* a Portuguese and Spanish form of **Xavier**.

Jay *masc* a surname, meaning jay, the bird, used as a first name (*Old French*); *masc, fem* a diminutive form for names beginning with *J*.

Jayne *fem* a variant form of **Jane**.

Jean[1] *fem* a variant form of **Jane**; a diminutive form is **Jeanie**.

Jean[2] *masc* the French form of **John**.

Jeanette, Jeannette *fem* a diminutive form of **Jeanne**, now used independently as an English-language name.

Jeanne *fem* the French form of **Jane**; a diminutive form is **Jeanette**.

Jedidiah *masc* beloved of the Lord (*Hebrew*); a

diminutive form is **Jed**.

Jefferson *masc* a surname, meaning son of Jeffrey or Geffrey, used as a first name (*Old English*).

Jeffrey, Jeffery *masc* district or traveller peace (*Germanic*); a variant form is **Geoffrey**; a diminutive form is **Jeff**.

Jehudi *masc* Jewish (*Hebrew*); a variant form is **Yehudi**.

Jehuda *fem* form of **Jehudi**; a variant form is **Yehuda**.

Jem, Jemmie, Jemmy *masc dimins.of* **James**.

Jemima, Jemimah *fem* dove (*Hebrew*); diminutive forms are **Mima, Mina**.

Jemma *fem* a variant form of **Gemma**.

Jenna, Jenni, Jennie *fem* diminutive forms of **Jane, Jennifer**, now used independently; a variant form is **Jenny**.

Jennifer, Jenifer *fem* the Cornish form of **Guinevere**; diminutive forms are **Jen, Jennie, Jenny**.

Jenny *fem* a diminutive form of **Jane, Jennifer**, now used independently; a variant form is **Jennie**.

Jeremia *fem* form of **Jeremiah**.

Jeremias *masc* a Spanish form of **Jeremy**.

Jeremy, Jeremiah *masc* Jehovah has appointed (*Hebrew*); a diminutive form is **Jerry**.

Jermaine *fem* a variant form of **Germaine**.

Jerome *masc* holy name (*Greek*); a diminutive form is **Jerry**.

Jérôme *masc* the French form of **Jerome**.

Jerónimo *masc* the Spanish form of **Jerome**.

Jerry *masc* a diminutive form of **Gerald, Gerard, Jeremy, Jerome**, now used independently.

Jerusha *fem* possessed; married (*Hebrew*).

Jervis *masc* a variant form of **Jarvis**.

Jess *fem* a diminutive form of **Jessica, Jessie**.

Jessamine, Jessamyn *fem* variant forms of **Jasmine**.

Jesse *masc* wealth (*Hebrew*).

Jessica *fem* God is looking (*Hebrew*); a diminutive form is **Jess**.

Jessie, Jessy *fem* diminutive forms of **Janet**, now used as names in their own right.

Jethro *masc* (*Hebrew*) superiority.

Jewel *fem* the name for a precious stone or valuable ornament used as a first name.

Jezebel *fem* domination (*Hebrew*).

Jill *fem* a diminutive form of **Gillian, Jillian**, now used independently.

Jillian *fem* form of **Julian**; diminutive forms are **Jill, Jilly**.

Jim, Jimmie, Jimmy *masc* diminutive forms of **James**.

Jo *masc* a diminutive form of **Joab, Joachim, Joseph**; *fem* a diminutive form of **Joanna, Joseph, Josepha, Josephine**.

Joab *masc* Jehovah is Father (*Hebrew*).

Joachim *masc* God has established (*Hebrew*).

Joan, Joann, Joanna, Joanne *fem* forms of **John**;
   diminutive forms are **Joanie, Joni**.

Joaquin *masc* the Spanish form of **Joachim**.

Job *masc* one persecuted (*Hebrew*).

Jobina *fem* form of **Job**.

Jocelyn, Jocelin *masc, fem* little Goth (*Germanic*);
   diminutive forms are **Jos, Joss**.

Jock, Jockie *masc* a diminutive form of **John**.

Jodie, Jody *fem* diminutive forms of **Judith**, now used
   independently.

Joe, Joey *masc* diminutive forms of **Joseph**.

Joel *masc* Jehovah is God (*Hebrew*).

Johan *masc* a Swedish form of **John**.

Johann *masc* a German form of **John**; a diminutive
   form is **Hans**.

Johanna *fem* the Latin and German form of **Jane**.

Johannes *masc* a Latin and German form of **John**.

John *masc* Jehovah has been gracious (*Hebrew*);
   diminutive forms are **Jack, Jackie, Jan, Jock,
   Johnnie, Johnny**.

Jolyon *masc* a variant form of **Julian**.

Jon *masc* a variant form of **John**; a diminutive form of
   Jonathan.

Jonah, Jonas *masc* dove (*Hebrew*).

Jonathan, Jonathon *masc* Jehovah gave (*Hebrew*); a
   diminutive form is **Jon**.

Joni *fem* a diminutive form of **Joan**.

Jordan *masc* flowing down (*Hebrew*); diminutive
forms are **Jud, Judd**.

Jordana *fem* form of **Jordan**.

Jorge *masc* the Spanish form of **George**.

Jos *masc* a diminutive form of **Joseph, Joshua**; *masc,
fem* a diminutive form of **Jocelyn, Jocelin**.

Joscelin *masc, fem* a French form of **Jocelyn**.

Josceline *fem* form of **Jocelyn**.

José *masc* the Spanish form of **Joseph**; diminutive
forms are **Pepe, Pepillo, Pepiro**.

Josef *masc* a German form of **Joseph**.

Josefa *fem* form of **Josef**.

Joseph *masc* God shall add (*Hebrew*); diminutive forms
are **Jo, Joe, Joey, Jos**.

Josepha *fem* form of **Joseph**.

Josephine *fem* form of **Joseph**; diminutive forms are
Jo, Josie, Phenie.

Josette *fem* a French diminutive form of **Josephine**,
now used independently.

Josh *masc* a diminutive form of **Joshua**, now used
independently.

Joshua *masc* Jehovah is salvation (*Hebrew*); a diminutive form is **Josh**.

Josiah, Josias *masc* Jehovah supports (*Hebrew*).

Josie *fem* a diminutive form of **Josephine**.

Joss *masc, fem* a diminutive form of **Jocelyn, Jocelin,
Joscelin**.

Joy *fem* the name of the feeling of intense happiness
used as a first name (*English*).

Joyce *fem* sportive (*Latin*).

Juan *masc* the Spanish form of **John**, now used as an
English-language form.

Juana *fem* the Spanish form of **Jane**; a diminutive form
is **Juanita**.

Judah *masc* confession (*Hebrew*); a diminutive form is
Jude.

Jud, Judd *masc* diminutive forms of **Jordan**, also used
independently.

Jude *masc* a diminutive form of **Judah**.

Judie, Judi *fem* diminutive forms of **Judith**, now used
independently.

Judith *fem* of Judah (*Hebrew*); diminutive forms are
Jodie, Judy.

Judy *fem* a diminutive form of **Judith**, now used
independently.

Jules *masc* the French form of **Julius**; a diminutive
form of **Julian, Julius**; *fem* a diminutive form of
Julia, Juliana.

Julia *fem* forms of **Julius**; a variant form is **Juliana**; a
diminutive form is **Julie**.

Julian *masc* sprung from or belonging to Julius (*Latin*);
a variant form is **Jolyon**.

Juliana *fem* form of **Julius**.

Julie, Juliet *fem* diminutive forms of **Julia**, now used

independently.

Julien *masc* the French form of **Julian**.

Julienne *fem* form of **Julien**.

Julieta *fem* a Spanish form of **Julia**.

Juliette *fem* the French form of **Julia**, now used as an English-language form.

Julio *masc* a Spanish form of **Julius**.

Julius *masc* downy-bearded (*Greek*).

June *fem* the name of the month used as a first name (*Latin*).

Juno *fem* queen of heaven, in Roman mythology the equivalent of **Hera** (*Latin*).

Justin *masc* the English form of *Justinus*, a Roman family name from **Justus** (*Latin*); a variant form is **Justinian**.

Justina, Justine *fem* forms of **Justin**.

Justinian, Justus *masc* variant forms of **Justin**.

Justus *masc* fair, just (*Latin*).

K

Kalantha, Kalanthe *fem* variant forms of **Calantha**.

Kalypso *fem* a variant form of **Calypso**.

Kane *masc* a surname, meaning warrior, used as a first name (*Irish Gaelic*).

Kara *fem* a variant form of **Cara**.

Karel *masc* the Czech and Dutch form of **Charles**.

Karen *fem* a Dutch and Scandinavian form of **Katherine**.

Karin *fem* a Scandinavian form of **Katherine**.

Karl *masc* a German form of **Charles**.

Karla *fem* form of **Karl**.

Karlotte *fem* a German form of **Charlotte**.

Karol *masc* the Polish form of **Charles**.

Karoline *fem* a German form of **Caroline**.

Karr *masc* a variant form of **Kerr**.

Kasimir *masc* peace (*Polish*).

Kaspar *masc* the German form of **Jasper**.

Kate *fem* a diminutive form of **Katherine**, also used independently.

Katerina *fem* a variant form of **Katherine**.

Kath, Kathie, Kathy *fem* diminutive forms of
  Katherine.
Katharina, Katharine *fem* German forms of
  Katherine; a diminutive form is **Katrine**.
Katherine *fem* pure (*Greek*); diminutive forms are
  Kate, Kath, Katie, Katy, Kay, Kit, Kittie.
Kathleen *fem* an Irish form of **Katherine**.
Kathryn *fem* an American form of **Katherine**.
Katie *fem* a diminutive form of **Katherine**, now used
  independently.
Katinka *fem* a Russian form of **Katherine**.
Katrine *fem* a diminutive form of **Katharina**; a variant
  form of **Katriona**; the name of a Scottish loch,
  meaning wood of Eriu, used as a first name.
Katriona *fem* a variant form of **Catriona**; a variant
  form is **Katrine**.
Katy *fem* a diminutive form of **Katherine**, now used
  independently.
Kavan *masc* a variant form of **Cavan**.
Kay *masc* giant (*Scots Gaelic*); *fem* a diminutive form
  of **Katherine**, now used independently; a variant
  form is **Kaye**.
Kayla, Kayleigh, Kayley *fem* derivation uncertain,
  possibly slender (*Irish Gaelic*), a combination of **Kay**
  and **Leigh**, or a variant form of **Kelly**.
Kean, Keane *masc* anglicized forms of **Cian**.
Kedar *masc* powerful (*Arabic*).

Keefe *masc* noble, admirable (*Irish Gaelic*).

Keegan *masc* a surname, meaning son of Egan, used as a first name (*Irish Gaelic*).

Keenan *masc* a surname, meaning little ancient one, used as a first name (*Irish Gaelic*).

Keir *masc* a surname, meaning swarthy, used as a first name (*Scots Gaelic*).

Keira *fem* a variant spelling of **Ciara**.

Keith *masc* a placename and surname, meaning wood, used as a first name (*Celtic*).

Keld *masc* a Danish form of **Keith**.

Kelly *fem* a surname, meaning descendant of war, used as a first name (*Irish Gaelic*).

Kelsey *masc* a surname, meaning victory, used as a first name (*Old English*).

Kelvin *masc* the name of a Scottish river, meaning narrow water, used as a first name (*Scots Gaelic*).

Kemp *masc* a surname, meaning warrior (*Old English*) or athlete (*Middle English*), used as a first name.

Ken *masc* a diminutive form of **Kendall, Kendrick, Kenelm, Kennard, Kennedy, Kenneth**.

Kendall, Kendal, Kendell *masc* a surname, meaning valley of the holy river, used as a first name (*Celtic/ Old English*); a diminutive form is **Ken**.

Kendra *fem* form of **Kendrick**.

Kendrick *masc* a surname, meaning hero, used as a first name (*Welsh*); a variant form is **Kenrick**; a diminutive form is **Ken**.

Kenelm *masc* royal helmet (*Germanic*) a diminutive
form is **Ken**.

Kennard *masc* a surname, meaning strong royal, used
as a first name (*Germanic*) a diminutive form is **Ken**.

Kennedy *masc* a surname, meaning helmeted or ugly
head, used as a first name (*Gaelic*); a diminutive form
is **Ken**.

Kennet *masc* a Scandinavian form of Kenneth; diminutive forms are **Ken, Kent**.

Kenneth *masc* fire-born; handsome (*Gaelic*); diminutive forms are **Ken, Kennie, Kenny**.

Kennie, Kenny *masc* diminutive forms of **Kenneth** and
other names beginning with Ken-.

Kenrick *masc* a variant form of **Kendrick**.

Kent *masc* a surname, meaning from the county of
Kent (meaning border), used as a first name (*Celtic*);
a diminutive form of **Kennet, Kenton**.

Kenton *masc* a surname, meaning settlement on the
river Kenn, or royal place, used as a first name (*Old
English*); diminutive forms are **Ken, Kent**.

Kenyon *masc* white-haired (*Gaelic*); a surname,
meaning mound of Ennion, used as a first name
(*Welsh*).

Kermit *masc* son of Diarmid (*Irish Gaelic*).

Kern *masc* dark one (*Gaelic*).

Kerr *masc* a Scottish form of the surname **Carr**, used as a first name; a variant form is **Karr**.

Kerry *fem, masc* the name of the Irish county used as a first name.

Kester *masc* a diminutive form of **Christopher**.

Keturah *fem* incense (*Hebrew*).

Kevin, Kevan *masc* comely, loved (*Irish Gaelic*); a diminutive form is **Kev**.

Kezia, Keziah *fem* the cassia tree (*Hebrew*); diminutive forms are **Kizzie, Kizzy**.

Kieran *masc* an anglicized form of **Ciaran**.

Kiernan *masc* a variant form of **Tiernan**.

Kim *fem* a diminutive form of **Kimberley**, also used independently.

Kimberley *fem* a surname, meaning wood clearing, used as a first name (*Old English*); a diminutive form is **Kim**.

King *masc* the title of a monarch or a surname, meaning appearance, or serving in a royal household, used as a first name (*Old English*); a diminutive form of names beginning with King-.

Kingsley *masc* a surname, meaning king's meadow, used as a first name (*Old English*).

Kingston *masc* a placename and surname, meaning king's farm, used as a first name (*Old English*).

Kinsey *masc* a surname, meaning royal victor, used as a first name (*Old English*).

Kirby *masc* a surname, meaning church village or

farm, used as a first name (*Old Norse*).

Kirk *masc* a surname, meaning one who lives near a church, used as a first name (*Old Norse*).

Kirkwood *masc* a surname, meaning church wood, used as a first name (*Old Norse/Old English*).

Kirsten *fem* a Scandinavian form of **Christine**.

Kirstie, Kirsty *fem* a diminutive form of **Kirstin**, now used independently.

Kirstin *fem* a Scots form of **Christine**; a diminutive form is **Kirstie.**

Kish *masc* a gift (*Hebrew*).

Kit *masc* a diminutive form of **Christopher, Kristopher;** *fem* a diminutive form of **Katherine**.

Kittie, Kitty *fem* diminutive forms of **Katherine**.

Kizzie, Kizzy *fem* diminutive forms of **Kezia**.

Klara *fem* the German form of **Clara**.

Klaus *masc* a variant form of **Claus**.

Klemens *masc* a German form of **Clement**.

Knight *masc* a surname, meaning bound to serve a feudal lord as a mounted soldier, used as a first name (*Old English*).

Knut *masc* a variant form of **Canute**.

Konrad *masc* a German and Swedish form of **Conrad**.

Konstanz *masc* the German form of **Constant**.

Konstanze *fem* the German form of **Constance**.

Kora *fem* a variant form of **Cora**.

Korah *masc* baldness (*Hebrew*).

Kris *masc* a diminutive form of **Kristoffer,**
 Kristopher.

Kristeen *fem* a variant form of **Christine**.

Kirstel *fem* a German form of **Christine**.

Kristen *masc* the Danish form of **Christian**, now also
 used in English as a girl's name.

Kristian *masc* a Swedish form of **Christian**.

Kristina *fem* the Swedish form of **Christina**.

Kristoffer *masc* a Scandinavian form of **Christopher**.

Kristopher *masc* a variant form of **Christopher**;
 diminutive forms are **Kit, Kris**.

Kurt *masc* a diminutive form of **Conrad**, now used
 independently; a variant form is **Curt**.

Kyle *masc* narrow (*Scots Gaelic*); the name of a region
 of southwest Scotland used as a surname.

Kylie *fem* a combination of **Kyle** and **Kelly**.

Kyrena *fem* a variant form of **Cyrena**.

L

Laban *masc* white (*Hebrew*).

Lachlan *masc* from the land of lakes (*Scots Gaelic*).

Lacey *masc, fem* a surname, meaning from Lassy in the Calvados region of Normandy, used as a first name (Old French).

Ladislao *masc* an Italian form of **Laszlo**.

Ladislas *masc* rule of glory (*Polish/Latin*).

Laszlo *masc* the Hungarian form of **Ladislas**.

Laetitia *fem* happiness (*Latin*); variant forms are **Latisha, Letitia**.

Laing *masc* a variant form of **Lang**.

Laird *masc* a Scots form of the surname Lord, meaning master, landowner (*Old English*), used as a first name.

Lalage *fem* chattering (*Greek-Latin*); a diminutive form is **Lallie, Lally**.

Lambert *masc* illustrious with landed possessions (*Germanic*).

Lamberto *masc* the Italian form of **Lambert**.

Lamond, Lamont *masc* a surname, meaning law giver,

used as a first name (*Old Norse/Scots Gaelic*).

Lana *fem* a variant form of **Alana**.

Lance *masc* land (*Germanic*); a diminutive form of **Lancelot**.

Lancelot *masc* a little lance or warrior; or a servant (*French*); a diminutive form is **Lance**.

Lander, Landor *masc* variant forms of the surname **Lavender**.

Lane *masc* a surname, meaning narrow road, lane, used as a first name (*Old English*).

Lang *masc* a Scottish form of the surname Long, meaning tall or long, used as a first name (*Old English*); a variant form is **Laing**.

Langford *masc* a surname, meaning long ford, used as a first name (*Old English*).

Langley *masc* a surname, meaning long meadow, used as a first name (*Old English*).

Lara *fem* a diminutive form of **Larissa** (*Latin*).

Laraine *fem* a variant form of **Lorraine**; the queen (*Old French*).

Larissa, Larisa *fem* meaning uncertain, possibly happy as a lark (*Greek/Russian*); diminutve forms are **Lara**, **Lissa**.

Lark *fem* the English word for a bird famed for rising early and for its song used as a first name.

Larry *masc* a diminutive form of **Laurence, Lawrence**.

Lars *masc* a Scandinavian form of **Laurence**.

Larsen, Larson *masc* son of Lars (*Scandinavian*).

Lascelles *masc* a surname, meaning hermitage or cell, used as a first name (*Old French*).

Latham, Lathom *masc* a surname, meaning barns, used as a first name (*Old Norse*).

Latimer *masc* a surname, meaning interpreter, used as a first name (*Old French*).

Latisha *fem* a variant form of **Laetitia**.

Laura *fem* laurel, bay tree (*Latin*); a diminutive form is **Laurie**.

Laurabel *fem* a combination of **Laura** and **Mabel**.

Laurel *fem* a name for the evergreen bay tree used as a first name.

Lauren *fem* form of **Laurence**; a variant form is **Loren**; a diminutive form is **Laurie**.

Laurence *masc* from Laurentium in Italy, place of laurels (*Latin*); a variant form is **Lawrence**; diminutive forms are **Larry, Laurie**.

Laurens *masc* a Dutch form of **Lawrence**.

Laurent *masc* the French form of **Laurence**.

Laurette *fem* a French form of **Laura**; a variant form is **Lauretta**.

Laurie *masc* a diminutive form of **Laurence**; a surname form of this used as a first name; variant forms are **Lawrie, Lawry**; *fem* a dimunitive form of **Laura, Lauren**.

Lavender *fem* the English name of the plant that bears blue or mauve flowers used as a first name; *masc* a surname, meaning launderer, used as a first name (*Old French*); a variant form is **Lander**.

Laverne *fem* the alder tree (*Old French*); diminutive forms are **Verna, Verne**.

Lavinia, Lavina *fem* of Latium in Italy (*Latin*).

Lawrence *masc* a variant form of of **Laurence**; diminutive forms are **Larry, Lawrie, Lawry**.

Lawrie, Lawry *masc* diminutive forms of **Lawrence**; a variant form of **Laurie**.

Lawson *masc* a surname, meaning son of Lawrence, used as a first name (*Old English*).

Lawton *masc* a surname, meaning from the place on the hill, used as a first name (*Old English*).

Layton *masc* a variant form of **Leighton**.

Lazarus *masc* destitute of help (*Hebrew*).

Lea *fem* a variant form of **Leah, Lee**.

Leah *fem* languid, or wild cow (*Hebrew*); variant forms are **Lea, Lee**.

Leal, Leale *masc* a surname, meaning loyal, true, used as a first name (*Old French*).

Leander *masc* lion man (*Greek*).

Leane *fem* a variant form of **Leanne, Liane**.

Leandre *masc* a French form of **Leander**.

Leandro *masc* an Italian form of **Leander**.

Leanne *fem* a combination of **Lee** and **Anne**; a variant form is **Leane**.

Leanora, Leanore *fem* German variant forms of
　　Eleanor.

Leda *fem* mother of beauty; in Greek mythology, a
　　queen of Sparta who was visited by Zeus (who
　　appeared to her in the form of a swan) and gave birth
　　to Helen (*Greek*).

Lee *masc fem* a surname, meaning field or meadow,
　　used as a first name (*Old English*); a variant form is
　　Leigh; *fem* a variant form of **Leah**.

Leif *masc* beloved one (*Old Norse*).

Leigh *masc* a variant form of **Lee**.

Leighton *masc* a surname, meaning herb garden, used
　　as a first name (*Old English*); a variant form is
　　Layton.

Leila *fem* night, dark (*Arabic*); variant forms are **Lela,
　　Lila, Lilah**.

Leith *masc* a placename, meaning moist place (*Celtic*)
　　or grey (*Scots Gaelic*), used as a first name.

Lela *fem* a variant form of **Leila**.

Leland *masc* a variant form of **Leyland**.

Lemuel *masc* devoted to God (*Hebrew*); a diminutive
　　form is **Lem**.

Len *masc* a diminutive form of **Leonard, Lennox,
　　Lionel**.

Lena *fem* a diminutive form of **Helena**, etc, also used
　　independently.

Lennard *masc* a variant form of **Leonard**.

Lennie *masc* a diminutive form of **Leonard, Lennox, Lionel**.

Lennox *masc* a placename and surname, meaning abounding in elm trees, used as a first name (*Scots Gaelic*).

Lenny *masc* a diminutive form of **Leonard, Lennox, Lionel**; a variant form is **Lonnie**.

Lenora *fem* a variant form of **Leonora**.

Leo *masc* lion (*Latin*); a variant form is **Leon**.

Leon *masc* a variant form of **Leo**.

Leona *fem* a variant form of **Leonie**.

Leonard *masc* lion strong (*Germanic*); a variant form is **Lennard**; diminutive forms are **Len, Lennie, Lenny**.

Leonarda *fem* form of **Leonard**.

Leonardo *masc* an Italian form of **Leonard**.

Leonhard *masc* a German form of **Leonard**.

Leonidas *masc* of a lion (*Greek*).

Leonie *fem* form of **Leo, Leon**; a variant form is **Leona**.

Leonora *fem* an Italian form of **Eleanor**; a variant form is **Lenora**; a diminutive form is **Nora**.

Leontine, Leontina *fem* form of **Leontius**.

Leontius *masc* of the lion (Latin).

Leontyne *fem* a variant form of Leontine.

Leopold *masc* bold for the people (*Germanic*).

Leopoldina, Leopoldine *fem* forms of Leopold.

Leopoldo *masc* an Italian and Spanish form of
   Leopold.

Leroy *masc* the king (*Old French*); a variant form is
   Elroy; diminutive forms are **Lee, Roy**.

Leslie *masc, fem* a surname, meaning garden by water,
   used as a first name (*Gaelic*).

Lesley *fem* form of Leslie.

Lester *masc* a surname, meaning from the Roman site
   (i.e. the present city of Leicester), used as a first name
   (*Old English*).

Leticia, Letitia *fem* variant forms of **Laetitia**.

Letizia *fem* an Italian form of **Laetitia**.

Lettice *fem* a variant form of **Laetitia**; diminutive
   forms are **Lettie, Letty**.

Lev *masc* a Russian form of **Leo**.

Levi *masc* joined (He*brew*).

Lewis *masc* bold warrior (*Germanic*); diminutive forms
   are **Lew, Lewie**.

Lex *masc* a diminutive form of **Alexander**.

Lexie, Lexy *fem* diminutive forms of **Alexandra**.

Leyland *masc* a surname, meaning fallow or untilled
   land, used as a first name (*Old English*); a variant
   form is **Leland**.

Liam *masc* the Irish form of **William**.

Liana, Liane, Lianna, Lianne *fem* sun (*Greek*); variant
   forms are **Leane, Leana, Leanna**.

Libby *fem* a diminutive form of **Elizabeth**.

Lidia *fem* an Italian and Spanish form of **Lydia**.

Liese *fem* a diminutive form of **Elisabeth**, now used independently.

Lil *fem* a diminutive form of **Lilian, Lily**.

Lila *fem* a variant form of **Leila**; a diminutive form of **Delilah**.

Lilac *fem* bluish (*Persian*), the English name of the syringa plant with fragrant purple or white flowers used as a first name.

Lilah *fem* a variant form of **Leila**; a diminutive form of **Delilah**.

Lili *fem* a variant form of **Lilie**.

Lilian *fem* a diminutive form of **Elizabeth**; a variant form of **Lily**; a variant form is **Lillian**.

Lilias, Lillias *fem* Scottish forms of **Lilian**.

Lilibet *fem* a diminutive form of **Elizabeth**.

Lilie *fem* a German form of **Lily**; a variant form is **Lili**.

Lilith *fem* of the night (*Hebrew*).

Lilli *fem* a variant form of **Lily**.

Lillian *fem* a variant form of **Lilian**.

Lily *fem* the name of the flowering plant with showy blossoms used as a first name; a variant form is **Lilli**; a diminutive form is **Lil**.

Lin *fem* a diminutive form of **Linda**.

Lina *fem* a diminutive form of **Selina** and names ending in -lina, -line.

Lincoln *masc* a placename and surname, meaning the place by the pool, used as a first name (*Celtic/Latin*).

Linda *fem* a diminutive form of **Belinda, Rosalind**, etc, now used independently; a variant form is **Lynda**; diminutive forms are **Lin, Lindie, Lindy**.

Lindall, Lindell *masc* a surname, meaning valley of lime trees, used as a first name (*Old English*).

Lindie *fem* a diminutive form of **Linda**.

Lindley *masc* a placename and surname, meaning lime tree meadow or flax field, used as a first name (*Old English*); a variant form is **Linley**.

Lindsay, Lindsey *masc, fem* a surname, meaning island of Lincoln, used as a first name; variant forms are **Linsay, Linsey, Linzi, Lynsay, Lynsey**.

Lindy *fem* a diminutive form of **Linda**.

Linford *masc* a surname, meaning from the ford of the lime tree or flax field, used as a first name (*Old English*).

Linley *masc* a variant form of **Lindley**.

Linnette *fem* a variant form of **Lynette**.

Linsay, Linsey *masc, fem* variant forms of **Lindsay**.

Linton *masc* a surname, meaning flax place, used as a first name (*Old English*).

Linus *masc* flaxen-haired (*Greek*).

Linzi *fem* a variant form of **Lindsay**.

Lionel *masc* young lion (*Latin*); a diminutive form is **Len**.

Lis *fem* a diminutive form of **Elisabeth**.

Lisa *fem* a diminutive form of **Elizabeth**, now used independently; a variant form is **Liza**.

Lisbeth *fem* a diminutive form of **Elisabeth**.

Lisette *fem* a diminutive form of **Louise**.

Lisle *masc* a surname, meaning island, or from Lisle in Normandy, used as a first name (*Old French*); variant forms are **Lyall, Lyle**.

Lissa *fem* a diminutive form of **Larissa, Melissa**.

Lister *masc* a surname, meaning dyer, used as a first name (*Old English*).

Litton *masc* a placename and surname, meaning loud torrent, used as a first name (*Old English*); a variant form is **Lytton**.

Livia *fem* a variant form of **Olivia**.

Liz *fem* a diminutive form of **Elizabeth**.

Liza *fem* a variant form of **Lisa**.

Lizbeth *fem* a diminutive form of **Elizabeth**.

Lizzie, Lizzy *fem* diminutive forms of **Elizabeth**.

Llewelyn *masc* lion-like (*Welsh*).

Lloyd *masc* a surname, meaning grey, used as a first name (*Welsh*).

Locke *masc* a surname, meaning enclosure, stronghold, used as a first name (*Old English*).

Logan *masc* a surname, meaning little hollow, used as a first name (*Scots Gaelic*).

Lois *fem* meaning uncertain, possibly good, desirable (*Greek*).

Lola *fem* a diminutive form of **Dolores, Carlotta**, now used independently.

Lombard *masc* a surname, meaning long beard, used as a first name (*Germanic*).

Lona *fem* a diminutive form of **Maelona**.

Lonnie *masc* a variant form of **Lenny**; a diminutive form of **Alonso**.

Lora *fem* a Welsh form of **Laura**.

Lorcan, Lorcán *masc* fierce (*Irish Gaelic*).

Lorelei *fem* the name of a rock in the River Rhine from where in German legend a siren lured boatmen.

Loren *fem* a variant form of **Lauren**.

Lorenz *masc* the German form of **Laurence**.

Lorenzo *masc* the Italian and Spanish form of **Laurence**.

Loretta *fem* a variant form of **Lauretta**.

Loring *masc* a surname, meaning man from Lorraine (bold and famous), used as a first name (*Germanic/ Old French*).

Lorn *masc* a variant form of **Lorne**.

Lorna *fem* a name invented by R. D. Blackmore, possibly from **Lorne**, for the heroine of his novel *Lorna Doone*.

Lorne *masc* a Scottish placename (the northern area of Argyll), of uncertain meaning, used as a first name; a variant form is **Lorn**.

Lorraine *fem* a surname meaning man from Lorraine

(bold and famous) used as a first name (*Old French*);
a variant form is **Laraine**.

Lot *masc* a veil; a covering (*Hebrew*).

Lotario *masc* the Italian form of **Luther**.

Lothaire *masc* the French form of **Luther**.

Lottie, Lotty *fem* diminutive forms of **Charlotte**.

Lotus *fem* the English name of a fruit that in Greek
mythology was said to induce langour and forgetful-
ness.

Lou *masc* a diminutive form of **Louis**; *fem* a diminutive
form of **Louisa, Louise**.

Louella *fem* a combination of **Louise** and **Ella**.

Louis *masc* the French form of **Lewis**; diminutive
forms are **Lou, Louie**.

Louisa *fem* form of **Louis**.

Louise *fem* the French form of **Louisa**, now used
widely as an English-language form; diminutive
forms are **Lisette, Lou**.

Lovel, Lovell *masc* a surname, meaning little wolf,
used as a first name (*Old French*); a variant form is
Lowell.

Lowell *masc* a variant form of **Lovel**.

Luc *masc* the French form of **Luke**.

Luca *masc* the Italian form of **Luke**.

Lucan *masc* a placename, meaning place of elms, used
as a first name (*Irish Gaelic*).

Lucas *masc* a variant form of **Luke**.

Luce *fem* a diminutive form of **Lucy**.

Lucia *fem* form of **Lucian**.

Lucian *masc* belonging to or sprung from Lucius (*Latin*).

Lucien *masc* a French form of **Lucian**.

Luciano *masc* an Italian form of **Lucian**.

Lucienne *fem* form of **Lucien**.

Lucifer *masc* light bringer (*Latin*).

Lucilla *fem* a diminutive form of **Lucia**.

Lucille, Lucile *fem* French forms of **Lucia**, now used as English-language forms.

Lucinda *fem* a variant form of **Lucia**; a diminutive form is **Cindy**.

Lucio *masc* a Spanish form of **Luke**.

Lucius *masc* from lux, light (*Latin*).

Lucrèce *fem* a French form of **Lucretia**.

Lucretia, Lucrece *fem* from lucrum, gain (*Latin*).

Lucretius *masc* form of **Lucretia**.

Lucrezia *fem* an Italian form of **Lucretia**.

Lucy *fem* a popular form of **Lucia**; a diminutive form is **Luce**.

Ludlow *masc* a placename, meaning hill by the rapid river, used as a first name (*Old English*).

Ludmila, Ludmilla *fem* of the people (*Russian*).

Ludovic, Ludovick *masc* variant forms of of **Lewis**; a diminutive form is **Ludo**.

Ludvig *masc* a Swedish form of **Lewis**.

Ludwig *masc* the German form of **Lewis**.

Luella *fem* a variant form of **Louella**.

Luigi *masc* an Italian form of **Lewis**.

Luis *masc* a Spanish form of **Lewis**.

Luisa *fem* an Italian and Spanish form of **Louisa**.

Luise *fem* the German form of **Louisa**; a diminutive form is **Lulu**.

Lukas *masc* a Swedish form of **Luke, Lucas**.

Luke *masc* of Lucania in Italy (*Latin*).

Lulu *fem* a diminutive form of **Luise**.

Lundy *masc* a placename, meaning puffin island, used as a first name (Old Norse); born on Monday (*Old French*).

Lutero *masc* a Spanish form of **Luther**.

Luther *masc* illustrious warrior (*Germanic*).

Lyall *masc* a variant form of **Lisle**.

Lycurgus *masc* wolf driver (*Greek*).

Lydia *fem* of Lydia in Asia Minor (Gr*eek*).

Lyle *masc* a variant form of **Lisle**.

Lyn *fem* a diminutive form of **Lynette, Lynsay**.

Lynda *fem* a variant form of **Linda**; diminutive forms are **Lyn, Lynn, Lynne**.

Lynden, Lyndon *masc* a surname, meaning dweller by lime trees, used as a first name; a diminutive form is **Lyn**.

Lynette *fem* an English form of **Eluned**; variant forms are **Lynnette, Linnette**.

Lynn *fem* a diminutive form of **Lynda**, now used
   independently.

Lynn *masc* a surname, meaning pool or waterfall, used
   as a first name (*Celtic*); diminutive forms are **Lyn,
   Lin, Linn**.

Lynnette *fem* a variant form of **Lynette**.

Lynsay, Lynsey *masc, fem* variant forms of **Lindsay**.

Lyris *fem* She who plays the harp (*Greek*).

Lysander *masc* liberator (*Greek*); a diminutive form is
   Sandy.

Lysandra *fem* form of **Lysander**.

Lyss *masc* a diminutive form of **Ulysses**.

Lytton *masc* a variant form of **Litton**.

M

Maarten *masc* a Dutch form of **Martin**.

Mabel *fem* diminutive forms of **Amabel**, also used independently; a variant form is **Maybelle**.

Mabelle *fem* a French form of **Mabel**.

Madalena *fem* the Spanish form of **Madeleine**.

Maddalena *fem* the Italian form of **Madeleine**.

Maddie, Maddy *fem* diminutive forms of **Madeleine**.

Madeleine, Madeline *fem* from Magdala on the Sea of Galilee (*French*); a variant form is **Magdalene**; diminutive forms are **Maddie, Maddy, Mala**.

Madge *fem* diminutive forms of **Margaret, Marjory**.

Madison *masc* a surname, meaning son of Matthew or Maud, used as a first name (*Old English*).

Madoc *masc* good; beneficent (*Welsh*).

Madonna *fem* my lady, a title of the Virgin Mary (*Italian*).

Mae *fem* a variant form of **May**.

Maelona *fem* princess (Welsh); a diminutive form is **Lona**.

Maeve *fem* intoxicating (*Celtic*); variant forms are **Mave, Meave**.

Magda *fem* a German and Scandinavian form of
   Magdalene.

Magdalene, Magdalen *fem* variant forms of
   Madeleine.

Magee *masc* a surname, meaning son of Hugh, used a a
   first name (*Irish Gaelic*); a variant form is **McGee**.

Maggie *fem* diminutive forms of **Margaret**.

Magnolia *fem* the name of a tree with showy flowers,
   named after the French botanist Pierre Magnol, used
   as a first name.

Magnus *masc* great (*Latin*).

Mahalia *fem* tenderness (*Hebrew*).

Mai, Mair *fem* Welsh forms of **May**.

Maida *fem* the name of a place in Calabria in Spain,
   where a battle was fought in 1806, used as a first
   name; a diminutive form is **Maidie**.

Mairead *fem* an Irish form of **Margaret**.

Mairi *fem* Scots Gaelic form of **Mary**.

Maisie *fem* diminutive forms of **Margaret**, also used
   independently.

Maitland *masc* a surname, meaning unproductive land,
   used as a first name (*Old French*).

Makepeace *masc* a surname, meaning peacemaker,
   used as a first name (*Old English*).

Mala *fem* a diminutive form of **Madeleine**.

Malachi *masc* messenger of Jehovah (*Hebrew*).

Malcolm *masc* servant of Columba (*Scots Gaelic*);

diminutive forms are **Calum, Mal**.

Malise *masc* servant of Jesus (*Scots Gaelic*).

Mallory *masc* a surname, meaning unfortunate, luckless, used as a first name (*Old French*).

Malone *masc* a surname, meaning follower of St John, used as a first name (*Irish Gaelic*).

Malvina *fem* smooth brow (*Scots Gaelic*).

Mame, Mamie *fem* diminutive forms of **Mary**, now used independently.

Manasseh *masc* one who causes to forget (*Hebrew*).

Manda *fem* a diminutive form of **Amanda**.

Mandy *fem* diminutive forms of **Amanda, Miranda**, now used independently; *masc* little man (*German*).

Manette *fem* a French form of **Mary**.

Manfred *masc* man of peace (*Germanic*); a diminutive form is **Manny**.

Manfredi *masc* the Italian form of **Manfred**.

Manfried *masc* a German form of **Manfred**.

Manley *masc* a surname, meaning brave, upright, used as a first name (*Middle English*).

Manny *masc* diminutive forms of **Emmnauel, Immanuel, Manfred**.

Manuel *masc* the Spanish form of **Emmanuel**.

Manuela *fem* God with us (*Spanish*).

Marc *masc* a French form of **Mark**; a variant form of **Marcus**.

Marcel *masc* a French form of **Marcellus**.

Marcela *fem* a Spanish form of **Marcella**.

Marcella *fem* form of **Marcellus**.

Marcelle *fem* a French form of **Marcella**.

Marcello *masc* the Italian form of **Marcel**.

Marcellus *masc* the Latin and Scots Gaelic form of **Mark**.

Marcelo *masc* a Spanish form of **Marcel**.

Marcia *fem* form of **Marcius**; a variant form is **Marsha**; diminutive forms are **Marcie, Marcy**.

Marcius *masc* a variant form of **Mark**.

Marco *masc* the Italian form of **Mark**.

Marcos *masc* the Spanish form of **Mark**.

Marcus *masc* the Latin form of **Mark**, now used as an English variant form; a variant form is **Marc**.

Mared *fem* a Welsh form of **Margaret**.

Margaret *fem* a pearl (*Greek*); diminutive forms are **Greta, Madge, Maggie, Margie, May, Meg, Meggie, Meta, Peg**.

Margarete *fem* the Danish and German form of **Margaret**; diminutive forms are **Grete, Gretchen**.

Margaretha *fem* a Dutch form of **Margaret**.

Margarita *fem* the Spanish form of **Margaret**; a diminutive form is **Rita**.

Margaux *fem* a variant form of **Margot**.

Margery *fem* in the Middle Ages a diminutive form of **Margaret**, but now a name in its own right; a variant form is **Marjorie**; a diminutive form is **Madge, Marge**.

Margherita *fem* the Italian form of **Margaret**; a diminutive form is **Rita**.

Margie *fem* diminutive form of **Margaret**.

Margo, Margot *fem* diminutive forms of **Margaret, Marguerite**, now used independently; a variant form is **Margaux**.

Marguerite *fem* the French form of **Margaret**; diminutive forms are **Margo, Margot**.

Mari *fem* an Irish and Welsh form of **Mary**.

Maria *fem* the Latin, Italian, German, and Spanish forms of **Mary**; a diminutive form is **Ria**.

Mariam *fem* the Greek form of **Mary**.

Marian *fem* a French form of **Marion**.

Marianna *fem* an Italian form of **Marianne, Marion**.

Marianne *fem* a French and German form of **Marion**; a compound of **Mary** and **Ann**.

Maribella *fem* a compound of **Mary** and **Bella**.

Marie *fem* a French form of **Mary**; a diminutive form is **Marion**.

Marietta *fem* diminutive form of **Maria**, also used independently

Marigold *fem* the name of the golden flower used as a first name.

Marilyn *fem* diminutive form of **Mary**, also used independently.

Marina *fem* of the sea (*Latin*).

Mario *masc* an Italian form of **Marius**.

Marion *fem* a variant form of **Mary**; *masc* a French
form of **Mary**, in compliment to the Virgin Mary.

Marisa *fem* summit (*Hebrew*).

Marius *masc* martial (*Latin*).

Marjorie, Marjory *fem* variant forms of **Margery**.

Mark *masc* a hammer; a male; sprung from Mars
(*Latin*); a variant form is **Marcus**.

Markus *masc* the German and Sweidsh form of **Mark**.

Marland *masc* a surname, meaning lake land, used as a
first name (*Old English*).

Marlene *fem* a contraction of **Maria Magdalena**
(*German*).

Marlo *masc* a variant form of **Marlow**.

Marlon *masc* of uncertain meaning, possibly hawk-like
(*French*).

Marlow *masc* a placename and surname, meaning land
of the former pool, used as a first name (*Old English*); variant forms are **Marlo, Marlowe**.

Marmaduke *masc* a mighty noble; Madoc's servant
(*Celtic*); a diminutive form is **Duke**.

Marmion *masc* a surname, meaning brat, monkey, used
as a first name (*Old French*).

Marsden *masc* a surname, meaning boundary valley,
used as a first name (*Old English*).

Marsh *masc* a surname, meaning marsh, used as a first
name (*Old English*).

Marsha *fem* a variant form of **Marcia**.

Marshall *masc* a surname, meaning horse servant, used as a first name (*Germanic*).

Marston *masc* a surname, meaning place by a marsh, used as a first name (*Old English*).

Marta *fem* the Italian, Spanish and Swedish form of **Martha**, now used as an English-language form; a variant form is **Martita**.

Martha *fem* lady (*Hebrew*); diminutive forms are **Mat**, **Mattie**.

Marthe *fem* the French and German form of **Martha**.

Marti *fem* a diminutive form of **Martina**, **Martine**.

Martijn *masc* a Dutch form of **Martin**.

Martin *masc* of Mars; warlike (*Latin*); a variant form is **Martyn**; a diminutive form is **Marty**.

Martina *fem* forms of **Martin**; a diminutive form is **Marti**.

Martine *fem* the French form of **Martina**, now used as an English-language form; a diminutive form is **Marti**.

Martino *masc* an Italian and Spanish form of **Martin**.

Martita *fem* a variant form of **Marta**; a diminutive form is **Tita**.

Marty *masc* a diminutive form of **Martin**.

Martyn *masc* a variant form of **Martin**.

Marvin *masc* a variant form of **Mervin**.

Marwood *masc* a surname, meaning bigger or boundary wood, used as a first name (*Old English*).

Mary *fem* bitter; their rebellion; star of the sea (*Hebrew*); variant forms are **Marion, Miriam**; diminutive forms are **Mamie, May, Minnie, Mollie, Polly**.

Maryann, Maryanne *fem* compounds of **Mary** and **Ann** or **Anne**.

Marylou *fem* a compound of **Mary** and **Louise**.

Massimiliano *masc* the Italian form of **Maximilian**.

Mat *masc* a diminutive form of **Matthew**; *fem* a diminutive form of **Martha, Mathilda**.

Mateo *masc* the Spanish form of **Matthew**.

Mather *masc* a surname, meaning mower, used as a first name (*Old English*).

Matheson, Mathieson *masc* a surname, meaning son of Matthew, used as a first name.

Mathias *masc* a variant form of **Matthias**.

Mathieu *masc* a French form of **Matthew**.

Mathilda *fem* a variant form of **Matilda**.

Mathilde *fem* the French form of **Matilda**.

Matilda *fem* might war (Germanic); a variant form is **Mathilda**; diminutive forms are **Mat, Mattie, Tilda, Tilly**.

Matilde *fem* the Italian and Spanish form of **Matilda**.

Matt *masc* a diminutive form of **Matthew**.

Mattaeus *masc* a Danish form of **Matthew**.

Matteo *masc* the Italian form of **Matthew**.

Matthais *masc* a Greek form of **Matthew**.

Matthäus *masc* a German form of **Matthew**.

Mattheus *masc* a Dutch and Swedish form of **Matthew**.

Matthew *masc* gift of Jehovah (*Hebrew*); diminutive forms are **Mat, Matt, Mattie**.

Matthias *masc* a Latin form of **Matthew**; a variant form is **Mathias**.

Matthieu *masc* the French form of **Matthew**.

Mattie *fem* a diminutive form of **Matilda**; *masc* a diminutive form of **Matthew**.

Maud, Maude *fem* a medieval form of **Matilda**.

Maura *fem* an Irish form of **Mary**.

Maureen *fem* an Irish diminutive form of **Mary**.

Maurice *masc* Moorish, dark-coloured (*Latin*); a diminutive form is **Mo**.

Mauricio *masc* a Spanish form of **Maurice**.

Maurits *masc* a Dutch form of **Maurice**.

Maurizio *masc* an Italian form of **Maurice**.

Mauro *masc* the Italian form of **Maurus**.

Maurus *masc* from Mauritania, Moorish (*Latin*).

Mave *fem* a variant form of **Maeve**; a diminutive form of **Mavis**.

Mavis *fem* an alternative name of the song thrush used as a first name (*English*); a diminutive form is **Mave**.

Max *masc* a diminutive form of **Maximilian, Maxwell**, also used independently; a diminutive form is **Maxie**.

Maxie *masc* a diminutive form of **Max, Maximilian, Maxwell**; *fem* a diminutive form of **Maxine**.

Maximilian *masc* the greatest, a combination of
Maximus and *Aemilianus* (*Latin*); diminutive forms
are **Max, Maxie**.

Maximilien *masc* the French form of **Maximilian**.

Maxine *fem* form of **Max**.

Maxwell *masc* a surname, meaning spring of Magnus,
used as a first name; a diminutive form is **Max**.

May *fem* diminutive form of **Margaret, Mary**; the
name of the month used as a first name; a variant
form is **Mae**; a diminutive form is **Minnie**.

Maybelle *fem* a compound of May and Belle; a variant
form of **Mabel**.

Mayer *masc* a surname, meaning physician (*Old
French*) or farmer (*Germanic*), used as a first name;
variant forms are **Meyer, Myer**.

Maynard *masc* a surname, meaning strong, brave, used
as a first name (*Germanic*).

Mayo *masc* a placename, meaning plain of the yew
tree, used as a first name (*Irish Gaelic*).

McGee *masc* a variant form of **Magee**.

Meave *fem* a variant form of **Maeve**.

Medea *fem* meditative; in Greek mythology the princess who helped Jason obtain the Golden Fleece from
her father (*Greek*).

Medwin *masc* a surname, meaning mead friend, used as
a first name (*ld English*).

Meg, Meggie *fem* diminutive forms of **Margaret**.

Megan *fem Welsh* diminutive form of **Meg**, now used independently.

Mehetabel, Mehitabel *fem* benefited of God (*Hebrew*).

Meironwen *fem* white dairymaid (*Welsh*).

Mel *masc* a diminutive form of **Melville, Melvin, Melvyn**.

Melanie *fem* black (*Greek*).

Melbourne *masc* a surname, meaning mill stream, used as a first name (*Old English*).

Melchior *masc* of uncertain meaning, possibly king of light; in the Bible, one of the three kings (*Hebrew*).

Melchiorre *masc* the Italian form of **Melchior**.

Melfyn *masc* from Carmarthen (*Welsh*).

Melinda *fem* honey (*Greek*) plus the suffix -inda.

Melisande *fem* the French form of **Millicent**.

Melissa *fem* a bee (*Greek*); a diminutive form is **Lissa**.

Melody *fem* a word for tune or tunefulness used as a first name.

Melville, Melvin, Melvyn *masc* a surname, meaning Amalo's place, used as a first name (*Old French*); a diminutive form is **Mel**.

Mercedes *fem* the Spanish form of **Mercy** (as a plural),

Mercer *masc* a surname, meaning merchant, used as a first name (*Old French*).

Mercy *fem* the quality of forgiveness used as a first name (*English*).

Meredith *masc, fem* a surname, meaning lord, used as a

first name (*Welsh*).

Merfyn *masc* eminent matter (*Welsh*).

Meri *fem* a variant form of **Merry**.

Meriel *fem* a Welsh form of **Muriel**; variant forms are
   Merle, Meryl.

Merle *masc* blackbird (*Old French*); a variant form of
   Meriel.

Merlin, Merlyn *masc* sea fort (*Welsh*).

Merri, Merrie *fem* variant forms of **Merry**.

Merrill *masc* a surname, meaning son of Muriel
   (*Celtic*) or pleasant place (*Old English*), used as a
   first name; variant forms are **Meryl, Merryll**.

Merry *fem* the adjective, meaning cheerful, mirthful,
   joyous, used as a first name (*Old English*); a diminutive form of **Meredith**; variant forms are **Meri,
   Merri, Merrie**.

Merryll *masc* a variant form of **Merrill**.

Merton *masc* a surname, meaning farmstead by the
   pool, used as a first name (*Old English*).

Mervin, Mervyn *masc* a surname, meaning famous
   friend, used as a first name (*Old English*); a variant
   formis **Marvin**; anglicized forms of **Merfyn**.

Meryl *fem* a variant form of **Meriel, Merrill**.

Meta *fem* a diminutive form of **Margaret**.

Meyer *masc* a variant form of **Mayer**.

Mia *fem* a diminutive form of **Maria**.

Micah *masc* who is like unto Jehovah? (*Hebrew*).

Michael *masc* who is like unto God? (*Hebrew*);
  diminutive forms are **Mick, Micky, Mike**.

Michaela *fem* form of **Michael**.

Michaella *fem* the Italian form of **Michaela**.

Michel *masc* the French form of **Michael**; a German
  diminutive of **Michael**.

Michele *masc* the Italian form of **Michael**.

Michèle, Michelle *fem* French forms of **Michaela**, now
  used as English-language forms.

Mick, Micky *masc* diminutive forms of **Michael**.

Mignon *fem* a word, meaning sweet, dainty, used as a
  first name (*French*); a diminutive form is
  Mignonette; a diminutive form is **Minette**.

Miguel *masc* the Spanish and Portuguese form of
  Michael.

Mikael *masc* the Swedish form of **Michael**.

Mike *masc* a diminutive form of **Michael**.

Mikhail *masc* a Russian form of **Michael**; a diminutive
  form is **Mischa**.

Mil *fem* a diminutive form of **Mildred, Millicent**.

Milcah *fem* queen (*Hebrew*).

Mildred *fem* gentle counsel (*Germanic*); diminutive
  forms are **Mil, Millie**.

Miles *masc* a soldier (*Germanic*); a variant form is
  Myles.

Milford *masc* a placename and surname, meaning mill
  ford, used as a first name (*Old English*).

Miller *masc* a surname, meaning miller, grinder, used
   as a first name (*Old English*); a variant form is
   Milner.

Millicent *fem* work and strength (*Germanic*); a diminutive form is **Millie**.

Millie *fem* diminutive form of **Amelia, Emilia,
   Mildred, Millicent**.

Millward *masc* a variant form of **Milward**.

Milne *masc* a surname, meaning at the mill, used as a
   first name (*Old English*).

Milner *masc* a variant form of **Miller**.

Milo *masc* the Greek samson (*Greek*).

Milton *masc* a surname, meaning middle farmstead or
   mill farm, used as a first name (*Old English*); a
   diminutive form is **Milt**.

Milward *masc* a surname, meaning mill keeper, used as
   a first name (*Old English*); a variant form is
   Millward.

Mima *fem* a diminutive form of **Jemima**.

Mimi *fem* an Italian diminutive form of **Maria**.

Mimosa *fem* the English name of a tropical shrub with
   yellow flowers used as a first name, from imitative
   (*Latin*).

Minerva *fem* wise one; in Roman mythology the
   counterpart of Athena, goddess of wisdom.

Minette *fem* a diminutive form of **Mignonette**..

Minna, Minne *fem* love (*Germanic*); diminutive forms

of **Wilhelmina**.

Minnie *fem* a diminutive form of **Mary, May, Wilhelmina**.

Minta *fem* a diminutive form of **Araminta**.

Mira *fem* a diminutive form of **Mirabel, Miranda**.

Mirabel, Mirabelle *fem* wonderful (*Latin*); diminutive forms are **Mira, Myra**.

Miranda *fem* wonderful (*Latin*); diminutive forms are **Mira, Myra**.

Miriam *fem* variant form of **Mary**.

Mischa *masc* a diminutive form of **Mikhail**.

Mitchell *masc* a surname form of **Michael**; a surname, meaning big, great, used as a first name (*Old English*).

Mitzi *fem* a German diminutive form of **Maria**.

Mo *masc fem* diminutive form of **Maureen, Maurice, Morris**.

Modest *masc* the Russian form of *modestus*, obedient (*Latin*).

Modesty *fem* an English word from *modestus* (*Latin*) for the quality of being shy or humble used as a first name.

Modred *masc* counsellor; in Arthurian legend the knight who killed King Arthur (*Old English*).

Moira *fem* an anglicized Irish form of **Mary**; a variant form is **Moyra**.

Mollie, Molly *fem* diminutive forms of **Mary**, now used independently.

Mona *fem* noble (*Irish Gaelic*).

Monica *fem* of certain meaning, but possibly advising (*Latin*).

Monika *fem* the German form of **Monica**.

Monique *fem* the French form of **Monica**, now also used as an English form.

Monroe, Monro *masc* a surname, meaning mouth of the Roe river, used as a first name (*Irish Gaelic*); variant forms are **Munro, Munroe, Munrow**.

Montague, Montagu *masc* a surname, meaning pointed hill, used as a first name; a diminutive form is **Monty**.

Montgomery, Montgomerie *masc* a surname, meaning hill of powerful man, used as a first name (*Old French/Germanic*); a diminutive form is **Monty**.

Monty *masc* a diminutive form of **Montague, Montgomery**.

Morag *fem* great (*Scots Gaelic*).

Moray *masc* a variant form of **Murray**.

Morgan *masc fem* sea-dweller (*Celtic*).

Morgana *fem* form of **Morgan**.

Moritz *masc* the German form of **Maurice**.

Morley *masc* a surname, meaning moor meadow, used as a first name (*Old English*).

Morna *fem* a Scots variant form of **Myrna**.

Morrice, Morris *masc* variant forms of **Maurice**; a diminutive form is **Mo**.

Mortimer *masc* a surname, meaning dead sea, used as

a first name (*Old French*).

Morton *masc* a surname, meaning farmstead moor, used as a first name (*Old English*).

Morven *fem* a Scottish placename, meaning sea gap, used as a first name (*Scots Gaelic*).

Mosè *masc* the Italian form of **Moses**.

Moses *masc* meaning uncertain, most probably an Egyptian name (*Hebrew*)..

Moyra *fem a* variant form of **Moira**.

Muir *masc* a Scottish form of the surname Moore, meaning moor (*Old French*), used as a surname.

Muirne *fem* beloved (*Irish Gaelic*).

Mungo *masc* amiable (*Gaelic*).

Munro, Munroe, Munrow *masc* variant forms of **Monroe**.

Murdo, Murdoch *masc* sea-warrior (*Scots Gaelic*).

Muriel *fem* sea bright (*Celtic*).

Murray *masc* a surname, meaning seaboard place, used as a first name; a variant form is **Moray**.

Myer *masc* a surname, meaning marsh (*Old Norse*), used a first name; a variant form of **Mayer**.

Myfanwy *fem* my fine one (*Welsh*).

Myles *masc* a variant form of **Miles**; devotee of Mary (*Irish Gaelic*).

Myra *fem* a name invented by the poet Fulke Greville, possibly as an anagram of **Mary**, or to mean she who weeps or laments (*Greek*); a diminutive form of

   Mirabel, Miranda.
Myrna *fem* beloved (*Irish Gaelic*); a variant form is
   Morna.
Myron *masc* fragrant oil (*Greek*).
Myrtle *fem* the name of the shrub used as a first name.

N

Naamah *fem* pretty, loved (*Hebrew*).

Naaman *masc* pleasant (*Hebrew*).

Nadezhda *fem* hope (*Russian*).

Nadia *fem* an English, French and Italian form of
Nadezhda.

Nadine *fem* a French diminutive form of **Nadia**.

Nahum *masc* comforter (*Hebrew*).

Naida *fem* the water nymph (*Latin*); a diminutive form
is **Naiada**.

Nairn *masc* dweller by the alder tree (*Celtic*).

Nairne *fem* from the river (*Gaelic*).

Nan *fem* a diminutive form of **Ann, Nancy, Nanette**.

Nana *fem* a diminutive form of **Hannah**.

Nancy *fem* a diminutive form of **Ann**, now used
independently; diminutive forms are **Nan, Nina**.

Nanette *fem* a diminutive form of Ann, now used
independently; a diminutive form is **Nan**.

Naomi *fem* pleasantness (*Hebrew*).

Napea *fem* girl of the valley (*Latin*); diminutive forms
are **Napaea, Napia**.

Naphtali *masc* my wrestling (*Hebrew*).

Napier *masc* a surname, meaning linen keeper, used as a first name (*Old French*).

Napoleon *masc* lion of the forest dell (*Greek*); a diminutive form is **Nap**.

Nara *fem* nearest and dearest (*English*).

Narda *fem* fragrant perfume. The lingering essence (*Latin*).

Nash *masc* a surname, meaning ash tree, used as a first name (*Old English*).

Nat *masc* a diminutive form of **Nathan, Nathaniel**.

Natal *masc* the Spanish form of **Noël**.

Natale *masc* the Italian form of **Noël**.

Natalie *fem* a French form of **Natalya** now used as an English-language form.

Natalia *fem* a Spanish form of **Natalya**.

Natalya *fem* Christmas (*Latin/Russian*).

Natasha *fem* a Russian diminutive form of **Natalya**.

Nathan *masc* gift (*Hebrew*); a diminutive form is **Nat**.

Nathania *fem* gift of God (*Hebrew*); diminutive forms are **Natene, Nathene, Nathane**.

Nathaniel, Nathanael *masc* God gave (Hebrew); a diminutive form is **Nat**.

Neal, Neale *masc* variant forms of **Neil**.

Nebula *fem* a cloud of mist (*Latin*).

Ned, Neddie, Neddy *masc* (contraction of "mine Ed") diminutive forms of **Edgar, Edmund, Edward, Edwin**.

Nehemiah *masc* Jehovah comforts (*Hebrew*).

Neil *masc* champion (*Gaelic*); variant forms are **Neal, Neale, Nial, Niall**.

Nell, Nellie, Nelly *fem* diminutive forms of **Eleanor, Ellen, Helen**.

Nelson *masc* a surname, meaning son of Neil, used as a first name.

Nemo *masc* grove (*Greek*).

Nerice, Nerine, Nerissa *fem* from the sea (*Greek*).

Nero *masc* dark, black-haired (*Latin*).

Nerys *fem* lord (*Welsh*).

Nessa *fem* a diminutive form of **Agnes, Vanessa**.

Nessie *fem* a diminutive form of **Agnes**.

Nesta *fem* a Welsh diminutive form of **Agnes**.

Nestor *masc* coming home (*Greek*).

Netta, Nettie *fem* diminutive forms of **Henrietta**.

Neven *masc* a variant form of **Nevin**.

Neville *masc* a placename and surname, meaning new place, used as a first name (*Old French*).

Nevin *masc* a surname, meaning little saint, used as a first name (*Irish Gaelic*); variant forms are **Nevin, Niven**.

Newell *masc* a surname, meaning new field, used as a first name (*Old English*).

Newland *masc* a surname, meaning new land, used as a first name (*Old English*).

Newlyn, Newlin *masc* a placename and surname,

meaning pool for a fleet, used as a first name (*Cornish*).

Newman *masc* a surname, meaning newcomer, new settler, used as a first name (*Old English*).

Newton *masc* a surname, meaning new farmstead or village, used as a first name (*Old English*).

Nial *masc* variant forms of **Neil**.

Niamh *fem* bright (*Irish Gaelic*).

Niall *masc* a variant form of **Neil**.

Nickson *masc* a variant form of **Nixon**.

Niccolò *masc* an Italian form of **Nicholas**.

Nicholas *masc* victory of the people (*Greek*); a variant form is **Nicolas**; diminutive forms are **Nick, Nicky**.

Nick *masc* a diminutive form of **Nicholas, Nicol**.

Nicky *masc* a diminutive form of **Nicholas, Nicol**; *fem* a diminutive forme of **Nicole**.

Nicodemus *masc* conqueror of the people (*Greek*).

Nicol *masc* a Scottish surname form of **Nicholas** used as a first name.

Nicola *masc* an Italian form of **Nicholas**; *fem* a variant form of **Nicole**.

Nicolas *masc* a Spanish form of **Nicholas**.

Nicole *fem* form of **Nicholas**; variant forms are **Nicola, Nicolette, Colette**; diminutive forms are **Nicky, Nikkie**.

Nigel *masc* black (*Latin*).

Nikki *fem* a diminutive form of **Nicole**.

Nikolaus *masc* a German form of **Nicholas**.

Nils *masc* a Scandinavian form of **Neil**.

Nina *fem* a diminutive form of **Nancy**.

Ninette *fem French* a diminutive form of **Ann**.

Ninian *masc* meaning uncertain; the name of a 5th-century saint (*Celtic*).

Ninon *fem* a diminutive form of **Ann** (*French*).

Nita *fem* a diminutive form of **Anita, Juanita**.

Nixie *fem* Water sprite (*Germanic*); diminutive forms are **Nissie, Nissy**.

Nixon *masc* a surname, meaning son of Nicholas', used as a first name; a variant form is **Nickson**.

Noah *masc* rest (*Hebrew*).

Noble *masc* a surname, meaning noble, famous, used as a first name (*Old French*).

Noé *masc* the French and Spanish form of **Noah**.

Noè *masc* the Italian form of **Noah**.

Noël, Noel *masc .fem* Christmas (*French*)

Noëlle, Noelle *fem* form of **Noël**.

Nola *fem* famous (*Irish Gaelic*).

Nolan *masc* a surname, meaning son of the champion, used as a first name (*Irish Gaelic*)..

Noll, Nollie *masc* diminutive forms of **Oliver**.

Nona *fem* ninth (*Latin*).

Nora, Norah *fem* a diminutive form of **Eleanor, Honora, Leonora**, also used independently.

Norbert *masc* northern hero (*Germanic*).

Noreen *fem* an Irish form of **Nora**.

Norma *fem* a rule (*Latin*), but probably invented as the name of the heroine of Bellini's opera.

Norman *masc* northman (*Germanic*); a diminutive form is **Norrie**.

Northcliffe *masc* a surname, meaning north cliff, used as a first name (*Old English*).

Norton *masc* a surname, meaning northern farmstead or village, used as a surname (*Old English*).

Norville *masc* a surname, meaning north town, used as a first name (*Old French*).

Norvin *masc* northern friend (*Old English*).

Norward *masc* a surname, meaning northern guardian, used as a first name (*Old English*).

Norwell *masc* a surname, meaning northern stream, used as a first name.

Norwood *masc* a surname, meaning north wood, used as a first name (*Old English*).

Nowell *masc* an English form of **Noël**.

Nuala *fem* a diminutive form of **Fionnuala**, also used independently.

Nye *masc* a diminutive form of **Aneurin**.

O

Oakley *masc* a surname, meaning oak tree meadow, used as a first name (*Old English*).

Obadiah *masc* servant of Jehovah (*Hebrew*).

Obed *masc* serving God (*Hebrew*).

Oberon *masc* a variant form of **Auberon**.

Obert *masc* wealthy, brilliant (*Germanic*).

Octavia *fem* form of **Octavius**.

Octavie *fem* a French form of **Octavia**.

Octavius *masc* eighth (*Latin*).

Oda *masc* a French form of **Otto**.

Odd *masc* the Norwegian form of **Otto**.

Oddo, Oddone *masc* Italian forms of **Otto**.

Oded *masc* upholder (*Hebrew*).

Odelia, Odelie *fem* variant forms of **Odile**.

Odette *fem* a diminutive form of **Oda**.

Odile, Odille *fem* rich, wealthy (*Germanic*); variant forms are **Odelia, Odelie, Ottilie, Otilie**.

Odoardo *masc* an Italian form of **Edward**.

Ofra *fem* a variant form of **Ophrah**.

Ogden *masc* a surname, meaning oak valley, used as

first name (*Old English*).

Ogilvie, Ogilvy *masc* a surname, meaning high peak, used as a first name (*Celtic*).

Olaf, Olav*masc* divine remnant (*Old Norse*).

Oleg *masc* the Russian form of **Helge**.

Olga *fem* the Russian form of **Helga**.

Olimpia *fem* the Italian form of **Olympia**.

Olive *fem* an olive (*Latin*); a variant form is **Olivia**.

Oliver *masc* an olive tree (*Latin*); diminutive forms are **Ollie, Olly, Noll, Nollie**.

Oliverio *masc* the spanish form of **Oliver**.

Olivia *fem* a variant form of **Olive**; a diminutive form is **Livia**.

Oliviero *masc* the Italian form of **Oliver**.

Ollie, Olly *masc* diminutive forms of **Oliver**.

Olwen *fem* white track (*Welsh*).

Olympe *fem* the French form of **Olympia**.

Olympia *fem* heavenly (*Greek*).

Omar *masc* first son (*Arabic*).

Ona *fem* a diminutive form of names ending -ona, e.g. Fiona.

Onefre *masc* a Spanish form of **Humphrey**.

Onefredo *masc* an Italian form of **Humphrey**.

Onfroi *masc* a French form of **Humphrey**.

Onofrio *masc* the Italian form of **Humphrey**.

Onorio *masc* the Italian form of **Honorius**.

Oona, Oonagh *fem* variant forms of **Una**.

Opal *fem* the name of the iridescent gemstone used as a first name, precious stone (*Sanskrit*).

Ophelia *fem* from *ophis*, serpent (*Greek*).

Ophélie *fem* the French form of **Ophelia**.

Ophrah, Ophra *fem* fawn (*Hebrew*); variant forms are **Ofra, Oprah**.

Oprah *fem* a modern variant of **Ophrah**.

Oran *masc* pale-skinned man (*Irish Gaelic*); variant forms are **Orin, Orrin**.

Orazio *masc* the Italian form of **Horace**.

Oren *masc* laurel (*Hebrew*).

Oreste *masc* the Italian form of **Orestes**.

Orestes *masc* mountain climber; in Greek mythology the son of Agnamemnon, who killed his mother and her lover in revenge for the death of his father. (*Greek*).

Orfeo *masc* the Italian form of **Orpheus**.

Oriana, Oriane *fem* golden (*Latin*).

Oriel *fem* strife (*Germanic*).

Orin *masc* a variant form of **Oran**.

Orion *masc* son of light (*Greek*).

Orla *fem* golden girl (*Irish Gaelic*).

Orlanda *fem* form of **Orlando**.

Orlando *masc* the Italian form of **Roland**.

Ormond, Ormonde *masc* a surname, meaning from east Munster, used as a first name (*Irish Gaelic*).

Orna *fem* form or **Oran**.

Orpheus *masc* of undertain meaning; in Greek mythology, a poet who sought to retrieve his wife Eurydice from Hades.

Orrin *masc* a variant form of **Oran**.

Orso *masc* bear (*Latin/Italian*).

Orsola *fem* the Italian form of **Ursula**.

Orson *masc* little bear (*Latin/Old French*).

Ortensia *fem* the Italian form of **Hortense**.

Orville, Orvil *masc* golden place (*Old French*).

Orwin *masc* a variant form of **Erwin**.

Osbert *masc* god-bright (*Old English*); a diminutive form is **Ossie**.

Osborn, Osborne, Osbourne *masc* a surname, meaning divine bear, or warrior (*Germanic*) a diminutive form is **Ossie**.

Oscar *masc* divine spear (*Germanic*); a diminutive form is **Ossie**.

Oskar *masc* the German and Scandinavian form of **Oscar**.

Osmond, Osmund *masc* divine protection (*Germanic*); a diminutive form is **Ossie**.

Ossie *masc* a diminutive form of **Osbert, Osborn, Oscar, Osmond, Oswald**.

Osvaldo *masc* the Italian form of **Oswald**.

Oswald *masc* divine rule (*Germanic*).

Oswin *masc* god-friend (*Old English*).

Otis *masc* a surname, meaning son of Ote, used as a first name (*Germanic*).

Ottavia *fem* the Italian form of **Octavia**.

Ottavio *masc* the Italian form of **Octavius**.

Ottilie, Otilie *fem* variant forms of **Odile**.

Otto *masc* rich (*Germanic*).

Ottone *masc* an Italian form of **Otto**.

Owain *masc* a Welsh form of **Eugene**.

Owen *masc* a lamb; a young warrior (*Celtic*).

Oxford *masc* a placename, meaning ford for oxen, used as a first name (*Old English*).

Oxton *masc* a surname, meaning place for keeping oxen, used as a first name (*Old English*).

Oz, Ozzie, Ozzy *masc* diminutive forms of names beginning with *Os-*.

P

Pablo *masc* the Spanish form of **Paul**.

Paddy *masc* a diminutive form of **Patrick**; fem a diminutive form of **Patricia**.

Padraig *masc* the Irish Gaelic form of **Patrick**.

Paget, Pagett, Padget, Padgett *masc* a surname, meaning young page, used as a first name (*Old French*).

Paige, Page *fem* a surname, meaning page, used as a first name (*Old French*).

Palmiro *masc* palm (*Latin*).

Palmira *fem* form of **Palmiro**.

Paloma *fem* the Spanish word for dove used as a first name.

Pamela *fem* a name invented by the poet Sir Philip Sidney derived from the Greek work for honey; a diminutive form is **Pam**.

Pancho *masc* a diminutive form of **Francisco**.

Pandora *fem* gifted (*Greek*); in Greek mythology, the first woman on earth.

Pansy *fem* thought (*French*); the name of the garden

flower used as a first name.

Paola *fem* the Italian form of **Paula**.

Paolo *masc* the Italian form of **Paul**.

Pascal *masc* of the passover (*Latin/French*).

Pasquale *masc* the Italian form of **Pascal**.

Pat *masc* a diminutive form of **Patrick**; *fem* a diminutive form of **Patricia**.

Patience *fem* patience (*Latin*).

Patric *masc* a variant form of **Patrick**.

Patrice *masc* the French form of **Patrick**; *fem* the French form of **Patricia**.

Patricia *fem* form of **Patrick**; diminutive forms are **Paddy, Pat, Patsy, Pattie, Patty, Tricia**.

Patricio *masc* the Spanish form of **Patrick**.

Patricius *masc* a variant form of **Patrick**.

Patrick *masc* noble; a patrician (*Latin*); variant forms are **Patric, Patricius**; diminutive forms are **Paddy, Pat**.

Patrizia *fem* the Italian form of **Patricia**.

Patrizio *masc* the Italian form of **Patrick**.

Patrizius *masc* the German form of **Patrick**.

Patsy *fem* a diminutive form of **Patricia**.

Pattie, Patty *fem* diminutive forms of **Martha, Patience, Patricia**.

Paul *masc* little (*Latin*).

Paula *fem* form of **Paul**.

Paulette *fem* a French form of **Paula**.

Paulina, Pauline *fem* diminutive forms of **Paula**.

Payne, Payn *masc* a surname, meaning countryman, used as a first name (*Old French*).

Peace *fem* the word for the condition of tranquillity or calm used as a first name (*Latin*).

Pearl *fem* the name of the lustrous white gem used as a first name.

Pedaiah *masc* Jehovah ransoms (*Hebrew*).

Pedro *masc* the Portuguese and Spanish form of **Peter**.

Peer *masc* a Norwegian form of **Peter**.

Peg, Peggie, Peggy *fem* diminutive forms of **Margaret**.

Peleg *masc* division (*Hebrew*).

Penelope *fem* duck (*Greek*); diminutive forms are **Pen**, **Penny**.

Penny *fem* diminutive form of **Penelope**, now used independently.

Peony *fem* healing (*Greek*), the name of a plant with pink, red, white or yellow flowers used as a first name.

Pepe *masc* a diminutive form of **José**.

Pepin *masc* enduring (*Germanic*).

Pepillo, Pepito *masc* diminutive forms of **José**.

Per *masc* a Scandinavian form of **Peter**.

Percival, Perceval *masc* pierce valley (*Old French*).

Percy *masc* a surname, meaning from Perci-en-Auge in Normandy, used as a first name (*Old French*).

Perdita *fem* lost (*Latin*), invented by Shakespeare for a character in *The Winter's Tale*.

Peregrine *masc* wanderer (*Latin*); a diminutive form is **Perry**.

Peronel *fem* a contraction of **Petronel**.

Perry *masc* diminutive form of **Peregrine**, now used in its own right; a surname, meaning pear tree, used as a first name (*Old English*).

Persephone *fem* of uncertain meaning; in Greek mythology, goddess of the underworld (*Greek*).

Persis *fem* a Persian woman (*Greek*).

Peter *masc* stone (*Latin*); diminutive forms are **Pete, Peterkin**.

Petra *fem* form of **Peter**.

Petrina *fem* a diminutive form of **Petra**.

Petronel, Petronella *fem* form of Petronius, a Roman family name (*Latin*).

Petrus *masc* a German form of Peter.

Petula *fem* asking (*Latin*); a diminutive form is **Pet**.

Petunia *fem* the name of a plant with white, blue or purple flowers used as a first name.

Phebe *fem* a variant form of **Phoebe**.

Phedra *fem* bright (*Greek*).

Phèdre *fem* the French form of **Phedra**.

Phelim *masc* always good (*Irish*).

Phemie, Phamie *fem* diminutive forms of **Euphemia**.

Phenie *fem* a diminutive form of **Josephine**.

Phil *masc* a diminutive form of **Philip, Phillip**; *fem* a diminutive form of **Philippa**.

Philbert *masc* very bright (*Germanic*).

Philemon *masc* friendly (*Greek*).

Philip *masc* lover of horses (*Greek*); a variant form is
    Phillip; diminutive forms are **Phil, Pip**.

Philipp *masc* the German form of **Philip**.

Philippa *fem* form of **Philip**; diminutive forms are **Phil,
    Pippa**.

Philippe *masc* the French form of **Philip**.

Phillip *masc* a a variant form of **Philip**; diminutive
    forms are **Phil, Pip**.

Philomena *fem* love and strength (*Greek*).

Phineas, Phinehas *masc* serpent's mouth (*Hebrew*).

Phoebe *fem* moon (*Greek*); a variant form is **Phebe**.

Phyllida *fem* a variant form of **Phyllis**.

Phyllis *fem* a green bough (*Greek*).

Pia *fem* form of **Pio**.

Pierce *masc* a surname form of Piers used as a first
    name.

Pierre *masc* the French form of **Peter**.

Piers *masc* a variant form of **Peter**.

Pierse *masc* a surname form of Piers used as a first name.

Pieter *masc* a Dutch form of **Peter**.

Pietro *masc* the Italian form of **Peter**.

Pilar *fem* pillar (*Spanish*), an allusion to the Virgin
    Mary who appeared to St James the Greater standing
    on a pillar.

Pio *masc* the Italian form of **Pius**.

Pip *masc*. a diminutive form of **Philip, Phillip**; *fem* a diminutive form of **Philippa**.

Pippa *fem* a diminutive form of **Philippa**.

Pius *masc* holy (*Latin*).

Placido *masc* peaceful (*Latin/Spanish*).

Plato *masc* broad (*Greek*).

Polly *fem* diminutive form of **Mary**, now used independently.

Pollyanna *fem* a compound of **Polly** and **Anna**.

Pomona *fem* fruitful (*Latin*).

Poppy *fem* the name of the plant that has bright red flower used as a first name.

Portia *fem* gift (*Latin*).

Presley *masc* a surname, meaning priests' meadow, used as a first name.

Prima *fem* form of **Primo**.

Primo *masc* first born (*Latin*).

Primrose *fem* the name of the yellow spring flower used as a first name.

Priscilla *fem* from *prisca*, ancient (*Latin*); diminutive forms are **Cilla, Prissie**.

Prosper *masc* favourable, fortunate (*Latin*).

Pròspero *masc* the Italian form of **Prosper**.

Prudence *fem* the word for the quality of caution or circumspection used as a first name (*Latin*); diminutive forms are **Prue, Prudie**.

Prue *fem* a diminutive form of **Prudence, Prunella**.

Prunella *fem* plum (*Latin*); a diminutive form is **Prue**.

Psyche *fem* of the soul(*Greek*).

Pugh *masc* a surname, meaning son of Hugh, used as a
  first name (*Welsh*).

Q

Queenie *fem* a diminutive form of the word queen, the supreme woman, used as a first name (*Old English*).

Quenby *fem* a surname, meaning queen's manor, used as a first name (*Old English*).

Quentin *masc* fifth (*Latin*); a variant form is **Quinton**.

Querida *fem* beloved, a Spanish term of endearment used as a first name.

Quinta *fem* form of **Quinto**.

Quinto *masc* the Italian form of **Quintus**.

Quintus *masc* fifth (*Latin*).

Quenel, Quennel *masc* a surname, meaning queen war, used as a first name (*Old English*).

Quigley, Quigly *masc* a surname, meaning untidy, used as a first name (*Irish Gaelic*).

Quinby *masc* a variant form of **Quenby**.

Quincy, Quincey *masc* a surname, meaning fifth place, used as a first name (*Latin/French*).

Quinlan *masc* well formed (*Irish Gaelic*).

Quinn *masc* a surname, meaning wise, used as a first name (*Irish Gaelic*).

Quinton *masc* a variant form of **Quentin**.

R

Rab, Rabbie *masc* diminutive forms of **Robert**.

Raban *masc* raven (*Germanic*).

Rachel *fem* lamb (*Hebrew*); a variant form is **Rachelle**; diminutive forms are **Rae, Ray**.

Rachele *fem* the Italian form of **Rachel**.

Rachelle *fem* a variant form of **Rachel**.

Radcliffe *masc* a surname, meaning red cliff, used as a first name (*Old English*).

Radley *masc* a surname, meaning red meadow, used as a first name (*Old English*).

Radnor *masc* a placename and surname, meaning red slopes, used as a first name (*Old English*).

Rae *fem* a diminutive form of **Rachel**.

Rafe *masc* a variant form of **Ralph**.

Raffaele, Raffaello *masc* Italian forms of **Raphael**.

Rafferty *masc* a surname, meaning prosperous, used as a first name (*Irish Gaelic*).

Rahel *fem* a German form of **Rachel**.

Raimondo *masc* the Italian form of **Raymond**.

Raimund *masc* the German form of **Raymond**.

Raimundo *masc* a Spanish form of **Raymond**.

Rainaldo *masc* an Italian form of **Reginald**.

Rainier *masc* a French form of **Rayner**.

Raisa *fem* tolerant (*Greek*).

Raleigh *masc* a surname, meaning red or deer meadow, used as a first name (*Old English*); variant forms are **Rawley, Rayleigh**.

Ralph *masc* famous wolf or hero (*Germanic*); variant forms are **Rafe, Rolph**.

Ram *masc* height (*Hebrew*).

Ramón *masc* a Spanish form of **Raymond**.

Ramona *fem* form of **Ramón**.

Ramsden *masc* Ram's valley (*Old English*).

Ramsay, Ramsey *masc* a placename and surname, meaning wild garlic river island, used as a first name (*Old Norse*).

Ranald *masc* a variant form of **Reginald**.

Rand *masc* a diminutive form of **Randal, Randolf**.

Randal, Randall *masc* a surname diminutive form of **Randolph** used as a first name (*Old English*); a variant form is **Ranulf**.

Randolf, Randolph *masc* shield-wolf (*Germanic*); a variant form is **Ranulf**; diminutive forms are **Rand, Randy**.

Randy *masc* a diminutive form of **Randolf**, also used independently.

Ranee, Rani *fem* queen (*Hindi*).

Rankin, Rankine *masc* a diminutive surname form of
  Randolph used as a first name.

Ransom *masc* a surname, meaning son of Rand, used
  as a first name.

Ranulf *masc* a variant form of **Randolf**.

Raoul *masc* the French form of **Ralph**.

Raphael *masc* the healing of God (*Hebrew*).

Raphaela *fem* form of **Raphael**.

Raquel *fem* the Spanish form of **Rachel**.

Ras *masc* a diminutive form of **Erasmus, Erastus**.

Rasmus *masc* a diminutive form of **Erasmus**.

Rastus *masc* a diminutive form of **Erastus**.

Rawley *masc* a variant form of **Raleigh**.

Rawnsley *masc* a surname, meaning Raven's meadow,
  used as a first name (*Old English*).

Ray *masc* a diminutive form of **Raymond**, now used
  independently; *fem* a diminutive form of **Rachel**; a
  variant form is **Rae**.

Rayleigh *masc* a variant form of **Raleigh**.

Raymond, Raymund *masc* wise protection (*Germanic*); a diminutive form is **Ray**.

Rayne *masc, fem* a surname, meaning mighty army,
  used as a first name; variant forms are **Raine** (*fem*),
  Rayner (*masc*).

Rayner *masc* a variant form of **Rayne** (*Germanic*).

Rea *fem* a variant form of **Rhea**.

Read, Reade *masc* a surname, meaning red headed,

used as a first name(*Old English*); variant forms are
Reed, Reede.

Reading *masc* a placename and surname, meaning
people of the red one, used as a first name; a variant
form is **Redding**.

Reagan *masc* a variant form of **Regan**.

Reardon *masc* a variant form of **Riordan**.

Rebecca, Rebekah *fem* noose (Hebrew); diminutive
forms are Beckie, **Becky**.

Redding *masc* a variant form of **Reading**.

Redman *masc* a surname, meaning red cairn or
thatcher, used as a first name (*Old English*); a variant
form of **Redmond**.

Redmond *masc* counsel profection (*Germanic*); a
variant form is **Redman**.

Reece *masc* a surname form of **Rhys** used as a first
name.

Reed, Reede *masc* variant forms of **Read**.

Rees *masc* the English form of **Rhys**.

Reeve, Reeves *masc* steward, bailiff (*Old English*).

Regan *masc*, *fem* a surname, meaning little king, used
as a first name (*Irish Gaelic*); variant forms are
Reagan, Rogan.

Regina *fem* queen (*Latin*).

Reginald *masc* counsel rule (*Germanic*); diminutive
forms are **Reg, Reggie**.

Reilly *masc* a surname, meaning valiant, used as a first name (*Irish Gaelic*); a variant form is **Riley**

Reinald *masc* an early English form of **Reginald**.

Reine *fem* queen (*French*).

Reinhard *masc* a German form of **Reynard**.

Reinhold *masc* a Scandinavian form of **Reginald**.

Reinold *masc* a Dutch form of **Reginald**.

Remus *masc* power (*Latin*).

Renaldo *masc* a Spanish form of **Reginald**.

Renata *fem* a diminutive form of **Renée**.

Renato *masc* an Italian and Spanish form of **Reginald**.

Renatus *masc* the Latin form of **René**.

Renault *masc* a French form of **Reginald**.

René *masc* born again (*French*).

Renée *fem* form of **René**.

Renfrew *masc* a placename and surname, meaning
    point of the torrent, used as a first name (*Celtic*).

Rennie, Renny *masc* a diminutive surname form of
    Reynold used as a first name.

Renton *masc* a surname, meaning farmstead of Power,
    used as a first name (*Old English*).

Reuben *masc* behold a son (*Hebrew*); a diminutive
    form is **Rube**.

Reuel *masc* friend of God.

Reva *fem* form of **Reeve**.

Rex *masc* king (*Latin*).

Rexanne *fem* a compound of **Rex** and **Anne**; a variant
    form of **Roxanne**.

Reynard *masc* brave advice (*Germanic*); fox (*French*).

Reynold *masc* strong rule (*Germanic*).

Rhea, Rheia *fem* of uncertain origin and meaning; in Roman mythology she was the mother of Remus and Romulus; in Greek mythology she was the mother of several gods, including Zeus; a variant form is **Rea**.

Rhiain *fem* maiden (*Welsh*).

Rhiannon *fem* goddess (*Welsh*).

Rhoda *fem* rose (*Greek*).

Rhodri *masc* circle ruler (*Welsh*).

Rhona *fem* a variant form of **Rona**.

Rhys *masc* ardour (*Welsh*).

Ria *fem* a German diminutive form of **Maria**.

Rica *fem* a diminutive form of **Roderica**.

Ricardo *masc* a Spanish form of **Richard**.

Riccardo *masc* an Italian form of **Richard**.

Rich masc a diminutive form of **Richard, Richmond**.

Richard *masc* a strong king; powerful (*Germanic*); diminutive forms are **Dick, Rich, Richey, Richie, Rick, Rickie, Ricky, Ritchie**.

Richey, Richie *masc* diminutive forms of **Richard, Richmond**.

Richmond *masc* a surname, meaning strong hill, used as a first name (*Old French*); diminutive forms are **Rich, Richey, Richie**.

Rider *masc* a surname, meaning knight, rider, used as a first name (*Old English*).

Ridley *masc* a surname, meaning cleared meadow, used
as a first name (*Old English*).

Rigby *masc* a surname, meaning farm on a ridge, used
as first name (*Old English*).

Rigg *masc* a surname, meaning at the ridge, used as a
first name (*Old English*).

Riley *masc* a variant form of **Reilly**.

Rina *fem* a diminutive form of names ending -rina.

Rinaldo *masc* an Italian form of **Reginald**.

Ring *masc* a surname, meaning wearing a ring, used as
a first name (*Old English*).

Riordan *masc* a surname, meaning bard, used as a first
name (*Irish Gaelic*); a variant form is **Reardon**.

Ripley *masc* a placename and surname, meaning strip-
shaped clearing, used as a first name (*Old English*).

Rita *fem* a diminutive form of **Margarita, Margherita**,
used independently.

Ritchie *masc* a diminutive and surname form of
Richard.

Ritter *masc* knight or rider (*Germanic*).

Roald *masc* famous ruler (*Old Norse*).

Robert *masc* bright in fame (*Germanic*); diminutive
forms are **Bob, Bobby, Rab, Rob, Robbie, Robby,
Robin**.

Roberta *fem* form of **Robert**.

Roberto *masc* the Italian and Spanish form of **Robert**.

Robin *masc, fem* a diminutive form of **Robert**, now

used independently; a variant form is **Robyn**.

Robina *fem* form of **Robin**.

Robinson *masc* a surname, meaning son of Robert, used as a first name (*Old English*).

Robyn *masc, fem* a variant form of **Robin**.

Rocco *masc* of uncertain meaning, possibly crow (*Germanic*).

Rochelle *fem* little rock (*French*).

Rochester *masc* a placename, and surname, meaning Roman fort at the bridges, used as a surname (*Old English*).

Rock *masc* stone or oak (*Old English*).

Rocky *masc* an English form of **Rocco**.

Rod *masc* a diminutive form of **Roderick, Rodney**.

Rodden *masc* a surname, meaning valley of deer, used as a first name (*Old English*).

Roddy *masc* a diminutive form of **Roderick, Rodney**.

Roderica *fem* form of Roderick; a variant form is **Rodericka**; a diminutive form is **Rica**.

Roderich *masc* the German form of **Roderick**.

Roderick, Roderic *masc* fame powerful (*Germanic*); diminutive forms are **Rod, Roddy, Rurik**.

Roderico *masc* an Italian form of **Roderick**.

Rodger *masc* a variant form of **Roger**.

Rodney *masc fem* a surname and placename, used as a first name; a diminutive form is **Rod**.

Rodolf *masc* an Italian and Spanish form of **Rudolph**.

Rodolphe *masc* a French form of **Rudolph**.

Rodrigo *masc* an Italian and Spanish form of
   Roderick.

Rodrigue *masc* the French form of **Roderick**.

Rogan *masc* a variant form of **Regan**.

Roger *masc* famous with the spear (*Germanic*); a
   variant form is **Rodger**.

Rogerio *masc* the Spanish form of **Roger**.

Rohan *masc* healing, incense (*Sanskrit*).

Rohanna *fem* form of **Rohan**.

Róisín, Roisin *fem* an Irish form of **Rose**.

Roland *masc* fame of the land (*Germanic*); variant forms
   are **Rolland, Rowland**; a diminutive form is **Roly**.

Rolanda, Rolande *fem* forms of **Roland**.

Roldán, Rolando *masc* Spanish forms of **Roland**.

Rolf *masc* a contraction of **Rudolf**; a variant form is
   Rollo.

Rolland *masc* a variant form of **Roland**.

Rollo *masc* a variant form of **Rolf**.

Rolph *masc* a variant form of **Ralph**.

Roly *masc* a diminutive form of **Roland**.

Roma *fem* a Roman (*Latin*).

Romeo *masc* a Roman (*Latin*).

Romilly *masc* a surname, meaning broad clearing (*Old
   English*) or place of Romilius (*Old French*), used as a
   first name

Romney *masc* a placename, meaning at the broad river,

used as a first name (*Old English*).

Ròmolo *masc* the Italian form of Romulus, of Etruscan origin and unknown meaning; in Roman legend, Romulus and his brother Remus founded Rome.

Romy *fem* a diminutive form of **Rosemary**.

Ron *masc* a diminutive form of **Ronald**.

Rona *fem* the name of a Scottish island, meaning rough rocky island, used as a first name (*Old Norse*); a variant form is **Rhona**.

Ronald *masc* a variant form of **Reginald**; diminutive forms are **Ron, Ronnie, Ronny**.

Ronalda *fem* form of **Ronald**; diminutive forms are **Ronnie, Ronny**.

Ronan *masc* little seal (*Irish Gaelic*).

Ronnie, Ronny *masc* diminutive forms of **Ronald**; *fem* diminutive forms of **Ronalda, Veronica**.

Rooney *masc* red, red-complexioned (*Gaelic*).

Rory *masc* red (*Irish and Scots Gaelic*).

Rosa *fem* a rose (*Latin*); diminutive forms are **Rosetta, Rosie**.

Rosabel, Rosabella, Rosabelle *fem* a compound of **Rosa** and **Bella**.

Rosalie, Rosalia *fem* little and blooming rose.

Rosalind, Rosaline *fem* beautiful as a rose (*Latin*); a diminutive form is **Linda**.

Rosamund, Rosamond *fem* horse protection; famous protection (*Germanic*); rose of the world (*Latin*).

Rosanne, Rosanna *fem* compounds of **Rose** and **Anne**; variant forms are **Roseanne, Roseanna**.

Roscoe *masc* a surname, meaning deer wood, used as a first name (*Old Norse*).

Rose *fem* the English form of **Rosa**; the name of the flower used as a first name; diminutive forms are **Rosette, Rosie**.

Roseanne, Roseanna *fem* variant forms of **Rosanne, Rosanna**.

Rosemarie *fem* a combination of **Rose** and **Marie**.

Rosemary *fem* the name of the plant associated with remembrance used as a first name; diminutive forms are **Romy, Rosie**.

Rosemonde *fem* a French form of **Rosamund**.

Rosetta *fem* a diminutive form of **Rosa**.

Rosette *fem* a diminutive form of **Rose**.

Rosh *masc* head (*Hebrew*).

Rosie *fem* a diminutive form of **Rosa, Rose, Rosemary**, now also used independently.

Roslin, Roslyn *masc, fem* a placename, meaning unploughable land by the pool, used as first name (*Scots Gaelic*); a variant form is **Rosslyn**.

Rosmunda *fem* the Italian form of **Rosamund**.

Ross *masc* a placename and surname, meaning promontory or moorland, used as a first name (*Scots Gaelic*).

Rosslyn *masc, fem* a variant form of **Roslin**.

Rowan *masc* red (*Irish Gaelic*).

Rowe *masc* a surname, meaning hedgerow, used as a first name (*Old English*).

Rowell *masc* a surname, meaning rough hill, used as a first name (*Old English*).

Rowena *fem* fame and joy (*Germanic*).

Rowland *masc* a variant form of **Roland**.

Rowley *masc* a surname, meaning rough meadow, used as a first name (*Old English*).

Roxanne, Roxane *fem* dawn of day (*Persian*); a variant form is **Rexanne**; a diminutive form is **Roxie**.

Roxburgh *masc* a placename and surname, meaning Rook's fortress, used as a first name (*Old English*).

Roy *masc* red (*Gaelic*); king (*Old French*).

Royal *masc* a variant form of **Royle**; *fem* the adjective meaning befitting a monarch, regal, used as a first name.

Royce *masc* a surname form of **Rose** used as a first name.

Royle *masc* a surname, meaning rye hill, used as a first name (*Old English*); a variant form is **Royal**.

Royston *masc* a surname, meaning place of Royce, used as a first name (*Germanic/Old English*).

Rube *masc* a diminutive form of **Reuben**.

Rubén *masc* a Spanish form of **Reuben**.

Ruby *fem* the name of the red gemstone used as a first name.

Rudi *masc* German diminutive form of **Rüdiger, Rudolf**.

Rüdiger *masc* the German form of **Roger**.

Rudolf, Rudolph *masc* famous wolf; hero (*Germanic*).

Rudyard *masc* reed enclosure (*Old English*).

Rufe *masc* a diminutive form of Rufus.

Rufus *masc* red-haired (*Latin*); a diminutive form is **Rufe**.

Rugby *masc* a placename and surname, meaning Hroca's stronghold, used as a first name (*Old English*).

Ruggiero, Ruggero *masc* Italian forms of **Roger**.

Rupert *masc* an anglicized Germanic form of **Robert**.

Ruprecht *masc* the German form of **Robert**.

Rurik *masc* a diminutive form of **Roderick, Roderic**.

Russell *masc* a surname meaning, red hair, used as a first name (Old French); a diminutive form is **Russ**.

Rutger *masc* a Dutch form of **Roger**.

Ruth *fem* friend (*Hebrew*).

Rutherford *masc* a surname, meaning cattle ford, used as a first name (*Old English*).

Rutland *masc* a placename, meaning Rota's estate, used as a first name (*Old English*).

Ruy *masc* a Spanish form of **Roderick**.

Ryan *masc* the Irish surname of uncertain meaning used as a first name.

Rye *masc* From the riverbank (*French*).

Rylan, Ryland *masc* a surname, meaning where rye grows, used as a first name (*Old English*).

S

Sabin *masc* a shortened form of **Sabinus**.

Sabina *fem* Sabine woman (*Latin*).

Sabine *fem* a French and German form of **Sabina**.

Sabino *masc* an Italian form of **Sabinus**.

Sabinus *masc* Sabine man (*Latin*); a shortened form is **Sabin**.

Sabra *fem* restful (*Hebrew*).

Sabrina *fem* of uncertain meaning, linked to the name of the River Severn (*pre-Celtic*); a variant form is **Zabrina**.

Sadie *fem* a diminutive form of **Sara**.

Sal *fem* a diminutive form of **Sally, Sarah**.

Salina *fem* From the salty place (*Greek*).

Sally, Sallie *fem* diminutive forms of **Sara**, now used independently.

Salome *fem* peaceful (*Hebrew*).

Salomon *masc* the French form of **Solomon**.

Salomo *masc* a Dutch and German form of **Solomon**.

Salomone *masc* the Italian form of **Solomon**.

Salvador *masc* Christ the saviour (*Latin/Spanish*).

Salvatore *masc* the Italian form of **Salvador**.

Salvia *fem* sage (*Latin*).

Sam *masc* a diminutive form of **Samuel**, now used
   independently; *fem* a diminutive form of **Samantha**.

Samantha *fem* meaning obscure, possibly listener
   (*Aramic*) or a compound of **Sam** and **Anthea**; a
   diminutive form is **Sam**.

Sammy *masc* a diminutive form of **Samuel**.

Samson, Sampson *masc* like the sun (*Hebrew*).

Samuel *masc* name of God, or heard by God (*Hebrew*);
   diminutive forms are **Sam, Sammy**.

Samuele *masc* the Italian form of **Samuel**.

Samuela *fem* form of **Samuel**.

Sancha, Sanchia *fem* variant forms of **Sancia**.

Sancho *masc* holy (*Spanish*).

Sancia *fem* form of **Sancho**; variant form are **Sancha,
   Sanchia**.

Sanders *masc* from Alexander (*Old English*); a diminutive form is **Sandy**.

Sandie *fem* a diminutive form of **Alexandra**.

Sandra *fem* a diminutive form of **Alessandra,
   Alexandra**, now used independently.

Sandy *masc* a diminutive form of **Alexander,
   Lysander, Sanders**; *fem* a diminutive form of
   Alexandra.

Sanford *masc* a surname, meaning sandy ford, used as
   a first name (*Old English*).

Sanson *masc* the German form of **Samson**.

Sansón *masc* the Spanish form of **Samson**.

Sansone *masc* the Italian form of **Samson**.

Santo *masc* saint (*Italian*).

Sapphire *fem* from *saphir*, beautiful (*Hebrew*); the name of the blue precious stone used as a first name.

Sarah, Sara *fem* princess (*Hebrew*); diminutive forms are **Sadie, Sal, Sally**.

Saul *masc* asked for by God (*Hebrew*).

Savanna *fem* a form of the word for an open grassland used as a first name (*Spanish*).

Saveur *masc* the French form of **Salvador**.

Saxon *masc* people of the short swords (*Germanic*).

Scarlett *fem* a variation of the word scarlet, a bright red colour, used as a first name by Margaret Mitchell in her novel *Gone with the Wind*.

Scott *masc* a surname, meaning of Scotland, used as a first name.

Sealey *masc* a variant form of **Seeley**.

Seamas, Seamus *masc* Irish Gaelic forms of **James**.

Sean *masc* an Irish Gaelic form of **John**.

Searle *masc* a surname, meaning armed warrior, used as a surname (*Germanic*).

Seaton *masc* a placename and surname, meaning farmstead at the sea, used as a first name (*Old English*); a variant form is **Seton**.

Sebastian *masc* august, majestic (*Greek*).

Sebastiano *masc* the Italian form of **Sebastian**.

Sébastien *masc* the French form of **Sebastian**.

Secondo *masc* the Italian form of **Secundus**.

Secundus *masc* second born (*Latin*).

Seeley *masc* a first name, meaning blessed and happy, used as a first name (*Old English*); a variant form is **Sealey**.

Seigneur *masc* a variant form of **Senior**.

Selby *masc* a placename and surname, meaning place by the willow trees, used as a first name (*Old English*).

Selden *masc* From the valley of the willow tree (*Old English*).

Selig *masc* blessed, happy one (*Yiddish*); a variant form is **Zelig**.

Selina, Selena *fem* parsley; heavenly (*Greek*); a diminutive form is **Lina**.

Selma *fem* form of **Anselm**.

Selwyn, Selwin *masc* wild (Old French) (*Germanic*).

Semele *fem* single (*Latin*).

Senga *fem* slender (*Gaelic*); backward spelling of **Agnes**.

Senior *masc* a surname, meaning lord, used as a first name (*Old French*); a variant form is **Seigneur**.

Seonaid *fem* a Gaelic form of **Janet**.

Septima *fem* form of **Septimus**.

Septimus *masc* seventh (*Latin*).

Seraphina, Serafina *fem* of the seraphim, of burning faith (*Hebrew*).

Serena *fem* calm; peaceful (*Latin*).

Serge *masc* the French form of **Sergius**.

Sergei *masc* the Russian form of **Sergius**.

Sergio *masc* the Italian form of **Sergius**.

Sergius *masc* a Roman family name of Etruscan origin and unknown meaning.

Sesto *masc* the Italian form of **Sextus**.

Seth *masc* appointed (*Hebrew*).

Seton *masc* a variant form of **Seaton**..

Seumas *masc* a Gaelic form of **James**.

Sewald, Sewall, Sewell, *masc* a surname, meaning sea powerful, used as a first name (*Old English*); a variant form is **Siwald**.

Sexton *masc* a surname, meaning sacristan, used as a first name (*Old French*).

Sextus *masc* sixth (*Latin*).

Seymour *masc* a surname, meaning from Saint-Maur in France, used as a first name (*Old French*).

Shalom *masc* peace (*Hebrew*).

Shamus *masc* an anglicized form of **Seamus**.

Shane *masc* an anglicized form of **Sean**.

Shanley *masc* a surname, meaning son of the hero, used as a first name (*Irish Gaelic*).

Shannon *fem* the name of the Irish river, meaning the old one, used as a first name.

Shari *fem* a diminutive form of **Sharon**.

Sharon *fem* a Biblical placename mentioned in the Song of Solomon used as a first name (*Hebrew*); a diminutive form is **Shari**.

Shaw *masc* a surname, meaning small wood or grove, used as a first name (*Old English*).

Shawn, Shaun *masc* anglicized forms of **Sean**.

Shea *masc* a surname, meaning stately, dauntless, used as a first name (*Irish Gaelic*).

Sheelagh *fem* a variant form of **Sheila**.

Sheelah *fem* petition (*Hebrew*); a variant form of **Sheila**.

Sheena *fem* an anglicized form of **Sine**.

Sheffield *masc* a placename, meaning open land by the Sheaf river, used as a first name (*Old English*).

Sheila, Shelagh *fem* anglicized forms of **Sile**; variant forms are **Sheelagh, Sheelah**.

Sheldon *masc* a surname, meaning heathery hill with a shed, flat-topped hill, or steep valley, used as a first name (*Old English*).

Shelley *fem* a surname, meaning clearing on a bank, used as a firrst name (*Old English*).

Shepard *masc* a surname, meaning sheep herder, shepherd, used as a first name (*Old English*).

Sherborne, Sherbourne *masc* a surname, meaning clear stream, used as a first name (*Old English*).

Sheree, Sheri *fem* variant forms of **Chérie**.

Sheridan *masc* a surname, meaning seeking, used as a
first name (*Irish Gaelic*).

Sherlock *masc* fair-haired (*Old English*).

Sherman *masc* a surname, meaning shearman, used as
a first name (*Old English*).

Sherwin *masc* a surname, meaning loyal friend or fast-
footed, used as a first name (*Old English*).

Sherwood *masc* a placename and surname, meaning
shore wood, used as a first name (*Old English*).

Sheryl *fem* a variant form of **Cheryl**.

Shirley *fem* a surname and placename, meaning thin
clearing, used as a first name; a diminutive form is
Shirl.

Sholto *masc* sower, seed-bearing (*Scots Gaelic*).

Shona *fem* the anglicized form of **Seonaid**.

Sian *fem* the Welsh form of **Jane**.

Sibeal *fem* an Irish form of **Sybyl**.

Sibyl, Sibylla *fem* soothayer (*Greek*); variant forms are
Sybyl, Sybylla; a diminutive form is **Sib**.

Siddall, Siddell *masc* a surname, meaning broad slope,
used as a first name (*Old English*).

Sidney *masc fem* a surname, meaning wide island, used
as a first name; a variant form is **Sydney**; a diminutive form is **Sid**.

Sidonia, Sidonie, Sydony *fem* of Sidon (*Latin*).

Siegfried *masc* victory peace (*Germanic*).

Siegmund *masc* the German form of **Sigmund**.

Sierra *fem* the name for a mountain range used as a
    first name (*Spanish*).

Sigismond *masc* the French form of **Sigmund**.

Sigismondo *masc* the Italian form of **Sigmund**.

Sigiswald *masc* victorious ruler (*Germanic*).

Sigmund *masc* victory protection (*Germanic*); a
    diminutive form is **Sig**.

Sigrid *fem* fair and victorious (*Old Norse*); a diminutive
    form is **Siri**.

Sigurd *masc* victorious guardian (*Old Norse*).

Silas *masc* a shortened form of **Silvanus**.

Sile *fem* the Gaelic form of **Celia, Cecily**, often ren-
    dered in English as **Sheila, Shelagh**, etc.

Silvain *masc* a French form of **Silvanus**.

Silvana *fem* form of **Silvano**.

Silvano *masc* the Italian form of **Silvanus**.

Silvanus *masc* of a wood (*Latin*); a variant form is
    Sylvanus.

Silvester *masc* of a wood (*Latin*); a variant form is
    Sylvester; a diminutive form is **Sly**.

Silvestre *masc* a French and Spanish form of **Silvester**.

Silvestro *masc* an Italian form of **Silvester**.

Silvia *fem* of a wood (*Latin*); a variant form is **Sylvia**.

Silvie *fem* the French form of **Silvia**.

Silvio *masc* the Italian and Spanish forms of **Silvanus**.

Sim *masc* a diminutive form of **Simon, Simeon**; *fem* a
    diminutive form of **Simone**.

Simon, Simeon *masc* hearing with acceptance (*Hebrew*); diminutive forms are **Sim, Simmy**.

Simona *fem* form of **Simon**; a diminutive form is **Sim**.

Simone *fem* the French form of **Simona**.

Sinclair *masc* a surname, meaning from St Clair in France, used as a first name (*Old French*); a variant form is **St Clair**.

Sine *fem* a Gaelic form of **Jane**, often rendered in English as **Sheena**.

Sinead *fem* an Irish Gaelic form of **Janet**.

Siobhan *fem* an Irish Gaelic form of **Jane**.

Sioned *fem* a Welsh form of **Janet**.

Sisley *fem* a variant form of **Cecily**; diminutive forms are **Sis, Sissie, Sissy**.

Siwald *masc* a variant form of **Sewald**.

Skelton *masc* a surname, meaning farmstead on a hill, used as first name (*Old English*).

Skerry *masc* sea rock (*Old Norse*).

Skipper *masc* a nickname and surname, meaning jumping (Middle English) or ship's captain (*Dutch*), used as a first name; a diminutive form is **Skip**.

Skipton *masc* a placename and surname, meaning sheep farm, used as a first name (*Old English*).

Slade *masc* a surname, meaning valley, used as a first name (*Old English*).

Sly *masc* a diminutive form of **Silvester, Sylvester**.

Smith *masc* a surname, meaning blacksmith, used as a

first name (*Old English*).

Snowden, Snowdon *masc* a surname, meaning snowy hill, used as a first name (*Old English*).

Sofie *fem* the French form of **Sophie**.

Sol *masc* the sun (*Latin*); a diminutive form of **Solomon**.

Solly *masc* a diminutive form of **Solomon**.

Solomon *masc* peaceable (*Hebrew*); diminutive forms are **Sol, Solly**.

Solveig *fem* house strong (*Old Norse*).

Somerled *masc* summer traveller (*Old Norse*).

Somerset *masc* a placename, meaning settlers around the summer farmstead, used as a first name (*Old English*).

Somerton *masc* a placename, meaning summer farmstead, used as a first name (*Old English*).

Somhairle *masc* an Irish and Scots Gaelic form of **Somerled**.

Sonya, Sonia *fem* a Russian diminutive form of **Sophia**.

Sophia *fem* wisdom (*Greek*).

Sophie, Sophy *fem* diminutive forms of **Sophia**, now used independently.

Sophronia *fem* of a sound mind (*Greek*).

Sorcha *fem* bright one (*Irish Gaelic*).

Sorley *masc* an anglicized form of **Somhairle**.

Sorrel *masc* sour (*Germanic*), the name of a salad plant used as a first name.

Spencer *masc* a surname, meaning steward or dispenser, used as a first name (*Old French*).

Spring *fem* desire (*Sanskrit*), the name of the season between winter and summer used as a first name.

Squire *masc* a surname, meaning shield bearer, used as a first name (*Old French*).

Stacey *masc* a diminutive form of **Eustace**, now used independently; fem a diminutive form of **Eustacia, Anastasia**, now used independently.

Stacy, Stacie *fem* diminutive forms of **Eustacia, Anastasia**, now used independently.

Stafford *masc* a surname, meaning ford by a landing place, used as a first name (*Old English*).

Stamford *masc* a variant form of **Stanford**.

Standish *masc* a surname, meaning stony pasture, used as a first name (*Old English*).

Stanford *masc* a surname, meaning stone ford, used as a first name (*Old English*); a variant form is **Stamford**.

Stanhope *masc* a surname, meaning stony hollow, used as a first name (*Old English*).

Stanislas, Stanislaus *masc* government and glory (*Slavonic*).

Stanley *masc* a surname and placename meaning stony field, used as a first name (*Old English*).

Stanton *masc* a surname, meaning stony farmstead, used as first name (*Old English*).

Star, Starr *fem* an English form of **Stella**.

Stasia *fem* a diminutive form of **Anastasia**.

Stefan *masc* a German form of **Stephen**.

Stefano *masc* the Italian form of **Stephen**.

Steffi, Steffie *fem* diminutive forms of **Stephanie**.

Stella *fem* star (*Latin*).

Stephan *masc* a German form of **Stephen**.

Stephanie *fem* form of **Stephen**; a diminutive form is **Stevie**.

Stephen, Steven *masc* crown (*Greek*); diminutive forms are **Steve, Stevie**.

Sterling *masc* a surname, meaning little star, used as a first name (*Old English*); a variant form is **Stirling**.

Stewart *masc* a variant and surname form of **Stuart**.

Stirling *masc* a variant form of **Sterling**; a placename, meaning enclosed land by the stream, used as a first name (*Scottish Gaelic*).

St John *masc* Saint John (pronounced *sinjon*).

Stockland *masc* a surname, meaning land of a religious house, used as a first name (*Old English*).

Stockley *masc* a surname, meaning cleared meadow of a religious house, used as a first name (*Old English*).

Stockton *masc* a placename and surname, meaning outlying farmstead, used as a first name (*Old English*).

Stoddard *masc* a surname, meaning horse keeper, used as a first name (*Old English*).

Stoke *masc* a placename and surname, meaning outlying farmstead, used as a first name (*Old English*).

Storm *masc, fem* the word for a meteorological condition of violent winds and rain, hail or snow used as a first name (*Old English*).

Stowe *masc* a surname, meaning holy place, used as a first name (*Old English*).

Strachan, Strahan *masc* a surname, meaning littl valley, used as a first name (*Scots Gaelic*).

Stratford *masc* a placename, meaning ford on a Roman road, used as a first name (*Old English*).

Stuart, Stewart, Steuart *masc* the surname meaning "steward" used as a first name (*Old English*).

Sukey, Sukie *fem* diminutive forms of **Susan**.

Sullivan *masc* a surname, meaning black-eyed, used as a surname (*Irish Gaelic*).

Summer *fem* season (*Sanskrit*), the name of the season between spring and autumn used as a personal name.

Sumner *masc* a surname, meaning one who summons, used as a first name (*Old French*).

Susan *fem* the English form of **Susanna**; diminutive forms are **Sue, Sukey, Sukie, Susie, Susy**.

Susanna, Susannah *fem* lily (*Hebrew*); a variant form is **Suzanna**.

Susanne *fem* a German form of **Susanna**.

Sutherland *masc* a placename and surname, meaning

southern land, used as a first name (*Old Norse*).

Sutton *masc* a placename and surname, meaning southern farmstead, used as a first name (*Old English*).

Suzanna *fem* a variant form of **Susanna**.

Suzanne *fem* a French and German form of **Susan**.

Sven *masc* lad (*Old Norse*).

Sybille *fem* the French form of **Sybyl**.

Sybyl, Sybilla *fem* variant forms of **Sibyl, Sibylla**; a diminutive form is **Syb**.

Sydney *masc* a variant form of **Sidney**.

Sylvain *masc* a French form of **Silvanus**.

Sylvanus *masc* a variant form of **Silvanus**.

Sylvester *masc* a variant form of **Silvester**; a diminutive form is **Sly**.

Sylvia *fem* a variant form of **Silvia**.

Sylvie *fem* the French form of **Silvia**.

T

Tabitha *fem* gazelle (*Aramaic*); diminutive forms are **Tab, Tabby**.

Tad *masc* a diminutive form of **Thaddeus**, also used independently.

Taddeo *masc* the Italian form of **Thaddeus**.

Tadhg *masc* an Irish Gaelic form of **Thaddeus**; a variant form is **Teague**.

Taffy *masc* Welsh form of David (*Celtic*).

Taggart *masc* a surname, meaning priest, used as a surname (*Scots Gaelic*).

Tate *masc* a surname, meaning cheerful, used as a first name (*Old Norse*); variant forms are **Tait, Teyte**.

Talbot *masc* a surname, meaning command of the valley, used as a first name (*Germanic*).

Talitha *fem* maiden (*Aramaic*).

Tallulah *fem* a placename, meaning spring water, used as a first name (*North American Indian*).

Tam *masc* (*Scots*) a diminutive form of **Thomas**.

Tamar *fem* palm tree (*Hebrew*); diminutive forms are **Tammie, Tammy**.

Tamara *fem* the Russian form of **Tamar**.

Tammie, Tammy *fem* diminutive forms of **Tamar, Tamsin**; *masc* a diminutive form of **Thomas**.

Tamsin *fem* a Cornish contraction of **Thomasina**, now used independently; a diminutive form is **Tammie**.

Tancredi, Tancredo *masc* Italian forms of **Tancred**.

Tancred*masc* thought strong (*Germanic*).

Tania, Tanya *fem* diminutive forms of **Tatiana, Titania**, now used independently.

Tanisha *fem* born on Monday (*Hausa*).

Tansy *fem* immortal (*Greek*), the name of a medicinal plant bearing yellow flowers used as a first name.

Tara *fem* a placename, meaning rocky assembly place, used as a first name; in Irish history, the site of ancient royal power (*Irish Gaelic*).

Tate *masc* a variant form of **Tait**.

Tatiana *fem* form of a Roman family name of unknown meaning (*Latin*); diminutive forms are **Tania, Tanya**.

Taylor *masc* a surname, meaning tailor, used as a first name (*Old French*).

Teague *masc* a variant form of **Tadhg**.

Tebaldo *masc* an Italian form of **Theobold**.

Ted, Teddie, Teddy *masc* diminutive forms of **Edward, Theodore, Theodoric**.

Tempest *fem* the word for a violent storm used as a first name (*Latin*).

Tennison, Tennyson *masc* variant forms of **Dennison**.

Teobaldo *masc* an Italian and Spanish form of
  Theobald.

Teodorico *masc* an Italian form of **Theodoric**.

Teodoro *masc* an Italian and Spanish form of
  Theodore.

Teodora *fem* an Italian and Spanish form of **Theodora**.

Teodosia *fem* an Italian form of **Theodosia**.

Terence *masc* from a Roman family name of unknown
  origin (*Latin*); variant forms are **Terrance, Terrence**;
  diminutive forms are **Tel, Terry**.

Terencio *masc* a Spanish form of **Terence**.

Teresa *fem* the Italian and Spanish forms of **Theresa**.

Terese *fem* a variant form of **Theresa**.

Teri *fem* a diminutive form of **Theresa**.

Terrance, Terrence *masc* variant forms of **Terence**.

Terri *fem* a diminutive form of **Teresa, Theresa**, now
  used independently.

Terris, Terriss *masc* a surname, meaning son of
  Terence, used as a first name.

Terry *fem* a diminutive form of **Teresa**; *masc* a diminutive form of **Terence**.

Tertius *masc* third (*Latin*).

Tess, Tessa, Tessie *fem* diminutive forms of **Esther,
  Teresa, Theresa**.

Teyte *masc* a variant form of **Tait**.

Thaddeus *masc* gift of God (*Greek-Aramaic*); diminutive forms are **Tad, Thad, Thaddy**.

Thaine *masc* a surname, meaning holder of land in return for military service, used as a first name (*Old English*); a variant form is **Thane**.

Thalia *fem* flourishing blossom (*Greek*).

Thane *masc* a variant form of **Thaine**.

Thea *fem* a diminutive form of **Althea, Dorothea**, now used independently.

Thecla *fem* god glory (*Greek*).

Thelma *fem* will (*Greek*).

Theda *fem* a diminutive form of **Theodora, Theodosia**.

Thelma *fem* a name coined in the 19th century by Marie Corelli for her novel *Thelma*, perhaps from wish (*Greek*).

Theo *masc fem* diminutive forms of **Theobald, Theodore, Theodora**.

Theobald *masc* bold for the people (*Germanic*); a diminutive form is **Theo**.

Theodor *masc* a Scandinavian and German form of **Theodore**.

Theodora *fem* form of **Theodore**; diminutive forms are **Dora, Theo**.

Theodore *masc* the gift of God (*Greek*); diminutive forms are **Ted, Teddie, Teddy, Theo**.

Theodoric, Theodorick *masc* people powerful (*Germanic*); diminutive forms are **Derek, Derrick, Dirk, Ted, Teddie, Teddy**.

Theodorus *masc* a Dutch form of **Theodore**.

Theodosia *fem* gift of God (*Greek*).

Theodosius *masc* form of **Theodosia**.

Theophila *fem* form of **Theophilus**.

Theophilus *masc* lover of God (*Greek*).

Theresa *fem* carrying ears of corn (*Greek*); diminutive forms are **Teri, Terri, Terry, Tess, Tessa, Tessie, Tracey, Tracie, Tracy**.

Thérèse *fem* the French form of **Theresa**.

Theresia, Therese *fem* German forms of **Theresa**.

Theron *masc* hero (*Greek*).

Thewlis *masc* a surname, meaning ill-mannered, used as a first name (*Old English*).

Thibaut *masc* a French form of **Theobald**.

Thierry *masc* a French form of **Theodoric**.

Thirza *fem* pleasantness (*Hebrew*); variant forms are **Thyrza, Tirza**.

Thomas *masc* twin (*Aramaic*); diminutive forms are **Tam, Thom, Tom, Tommy**.

Thomasina, Thomasine *fem* forms of **Thomas**.

Thor *masc* thunder (Old Norse), in Norse mythology, the god of thunder; a variant form is **Tor**.

Thora *fem* form of **Thor**.

Thorburn *masc* a surname, meaning Thor's warrior or bear, used as a first name (*Old Norse*).

Thordis *fem* a variant form of **Tordis**.

Thorndike, Thorndyke *masc* a surname, meaning thorny ditch, used as a first name (*Old English*).

Thorne *masc* a surname, meaning thorn tree or hawthorn, used as a first name (*Old English*).

Thorold *masc* Thor rule (Old Norse); a variant form is **Torold**.

Thorp, Thorpe *masc* a surname, meaning farm village, used as a first name (*Old English*).

Thorwald *masc* ruled by Thor (*Old Norse*); a variant form is **Torvald**.

Thurstan, Thurston *masc* a surname, meaning Thor stone, used as a first name (*Old Norse*).

Thyrza *fem* a variant form of **Thirza**.

Tib, Tibbie *fem Scots* diminutive forms of **Isabel, Isabella**.

Tibold *masc* a German form of **Theobald**.

Tiebout *masc* a Dutch form of **Theobald**.

Tiernan, Tierney *masc* a surname, meaning lord, used as a first name (*Irish Gaelic*); a variant form is **Kiernan**.

Tiffany *fem* the manifestation of God, the festival of Epiphany (*Greek*).

Tilda, Tilde *fem* diminutive forms of **Matilda**.

Till *masc* a German diminutive form of Dietrich.

Tilly *fem* a diminutive form of **Matilda**.

Tim *masc* a diminutive form of **Timon, Timothy**.

Timon *masc* reward (*Greek*).

Timothea *fem* form of **Timothy**.

Timothy *masc* honouring God (*Greek*); diminutive

forms are **Tim, Timmie, Timmy**.

Tina *fem* a diminutive form of **Christina, Christine**, etc, also used independently.

Tiphaine *fem* a French form of **Tiffany**.

Tiree *fem* the name of an island, meaning land of corn, used as a first name (*Scots Gaelic*).

Tirza, Tirzah *fem* variant forms of **Thirza**.

Tita *fem* form of **Titus**; a diminutive form of **Martita**.

Titania *fem* giant, in medieval folklore wife of Oberon and queen of fairies (*Greek*); diminutive forms are **Tania, Tanya**.

Titian *masc* an English form of **Titianus**.

Titianus *masc* a Roman name derived from **Titus**.

Tito *masc* the Italian and Spanish form of **Titus**.

Titus *masc* protected (*Latin*)

Tiziano *masc* the Italian form of **Titianus**.

Tobey *fem* form of **Toby**; a variant form is **Tobi**.

Tobi *masc* a variant form of **Toby**; *fem* a variant form of **Tobey**.

Tobias, Tobiah *masc* Jehovah is good (*Hebrew*); a diminutive form is **Toby**.

Toby *masc* a diminutive form of **Tobias**, now used independently; a variant form is **Tobi**.

Todd *masc* a surname, meaning fox, used as a first name (*Old Norse*).

Todhunter *masc* a surname, meaning foxhunter, used as a first name (*Old Norse/Old English*).

Tom *masc* a diminutive form of **Thomas**, now used
    independently.

Tomas *masc* the Spanish form of **Thomas**.

Tomasina, Tomina *fem* forms of **Thomas**.

Tomás *masc* a Spanish form of **Thomas**.

Tomaso, Tommaso *masc* Italian forms of **Thomas**.

Tommaso *masc* an Italian form of **Thomas**.

Tommie, Tommy *masc* diminutive forms of **Thomas**.

Toni *fem* diminutive forms of **Annette, Antoinette,
    Antonia**, now used independently.

Tonia *fem* a diminutive form of **Antonia**.

Tonie *fem* diminutive forms of **Annette, Antoinette,
    Antonia**, now used independently.

Tony *masc* a diminutive form of **Antony**; *fem* a diminu-
    tive form of **Annette, Antoinette, Antonia**.

Topaz *fem* the name of a white gemstone used as a first
    name topaz gem.

Tordis *fem* Thor's goddess (*Old Norse*); a variant form
    is **Thordis**.

Tormod *masc* Thor's spirit (*Old Norse*).

Torold *masc* a variant form of **Thorold**.

Torquil *masc* God's cauldron (*Old Norse*).

Tor *masc* a variant form of **Thor**.

Torr *masc* a surname, meaning tower (*Old English*) or
    bull (*Old French*) used as a first name.

Torvald *masc* a variant form of **Thorwald**.

Tory *fem* a diminutive form of **Victoria**.

Townsend, Townshend *masc* a surname, meaning end
of the village, used as a first name (*Old English*).

Tracey *masc* a variant form of **Tracy**; *fem* a diminutive
form of **Teresa, Theresa**.

· **Tracie** *fem* a diminutive form of **Teresa, Theresa**, now
used independently.

Tracy *masc* a surname, meaning Thracian, used as a
first name (*Old French*); a variant form is **Tracey**;
fem a diminutive form of **Teresa, Theresa**, now used
independently.

Traherne *masc* a surname, meaning iron strength, used
as a first name (*Welsh*).

Travers *masc* a surname, meaning crossing, crossroads,
used as a first name (*Old French*); a variant form is
Travis.

Traviata *fem* lead astray, the title of Verdi's opera used
as a first name (*Italian*).

Travis *masc* a variant form of **Travers**.

Tremaine, Tremayne *masc* a surname, meaning
homestead on the rock, used as a first name (*Cornish*).

Trent *masc* a river name, meaning liable to flood, used
as a first name (*Celtic*).

Trev *masc* a diminutive form of **Trevor**.

Trevelyan *masc* a surname, meaning mill farm, used as
a first name (*Cornish*).

Trevor *masc* a surname, meaning big river, used as a

first name (*Welsh*); a diminutive form is **Trev**.

Tricia *fem* a diminutive form of **Patricia**.

Trilby *fem* a name coined by George du Maurier in the 19th century for the heroine of his novel *Trilby*.

Trisha *fem* a diminutive form of **Patricia**.

Tristram, Tristam, Tristan *masc* grave; pensive (*Latin*); tumult (*Celtic*).

Trix, Trixie *fem* diminutive forms of **Beatrice**.

Troy *masc* a surname, meaning of Troyes, used as a first name (*Old French*); the name of the city in Asia Minor besieged by the Greeks used as a first name.

Truda, Trudie, Trudy *fem* diminutive forms of **Gertrude**.

True *masc* the adjective for the quality of being faithful and loyal used as a first name.

Truelove *masc* a surname, meaning faithful sweetheart, used as a first name (*Old English*).

Trueman, Truman *masc* a surname, meaning faithful servant, used as a first name (*Old English*).

Trystan *masc* a Welsh form of **Tristan**.

Tudor *masc* a Welsh form of **Theodore**.

Tuesday *fem* day of Mars (Old English), the name of the second day of the week used as a first name (*Old English*).

Tullio *masc* the Italian form of **Tullius**.

Tullius *masc* a Roman family name of Etruscan origin and uncertain meaning.

Tully *masc* a surname, meaning flood, used as a first name (*Irish Gaelic*); an English form of **Tullius**.

Turner *masc* a surname, meaning worker on a lathe, used as a first name (*Old French*).

Turpin *masc* a surname, meaning Thor the Finn, used as a first name (*Old Norse*).

Twyford *masc* a surname, meaning double ford, used as a first name (*Old English*).

Ty *masc* a diminutive form of **Tybalt, Tyler, Tyrone, Tyson**.

Tybalt *masc* a variant form of **Theobald**; a diminutive form is **Ty**.

Tye *masc* a surname, meaning enclosure, used as a first name (*Old English*).

Tyler *masc* a surname, meaning tile-maker, used as a first name (*Old English*); a diminutive form is **Ty**.

Tyrone *masc* a placename and surname, meaning land of Owen, used as a first name (*Irish Gaelic*); a diminutive form is **Ty**.

Tyson *masc* a surname, meaning firebrand, used as a first name (*Old French*); a diminutive form is **Ty**.

U

Uberto *masc* an Italian form of **Hubert**.

Uda *fem* form of **Udo**.

Udo *masc* prosperous (*Germanic*).

Udall, Udell *masc* a surname, meaning yew-tree valley, used as a first name (*Old English*).

Ugo, Ugolino, Ugone *masc* Italian forms of **Hugh**.

Ulises *masc* a Spanish form of **Ulysses**.

Ulisse *masc* an Italian form of **Ulysses**.

Ulmar, Ulmer *masc* wolf (*Old English*).

Ulric, Ulrick *masc* wolf power (*Old English*); the English form of **Ulrich**.

Ulrica *fem* English form of **Ulrike**.

Ulrich *masc* fortune and power (*Germanic*).

Ulrike *fem* form of **Ulrich**.

Ulysses *masc* wrathful (*Greek*)—*dimin* **Lyss**.

Umberto *masc* the Italian form of **Humbert**.

Una *fem* a lamb; hunger (*Irish Gaelic*); *fem* form of one (*Latin*) used by Edmund Spenser in *The Faerie Queene*.

Unity *fem* the quality of harmony or concord used as a

first name.

Unwin *masc* a surname, meaning not a friend, used as a surname (*Old English*).

Upton *masc* a surname, meaning upper farmstead, used as a first name (*Old English*).

Urania *fem* heavenly—the name of one of the muses (*Greek*).

Urbaine *masc* the French form of **Urban**.

Urban *masc* towm-dweller (*Latin*).

Urbano *masc* the Italian form of **Urban**.

Uri *masc* light (*Hebrew*).

Uriah *masc* fire of the Lord (*Hebrew*).

Urian *masc* a husbandman (*Danish*).

Uriel *masc* light of God (*Hebrew*).

Ursula *fem* she-bear (*Latin*).

Ursule *fem* the French form of **Ursula**.

Uzziah *masc* Jehovah is strength (*Hebrew*).

Uzziel *masc* God is strength (*Hebrew*).

V

Vachel *masc* little calf (*Old French*).

Vail *masc* a surname, meaning valley, used as a first name (*Old English*).

Val *masc* a diminutive form of **Valentine**; *fem* a diminutive form of **Valentina, Valerie**.

Valborga *fem* Protecting ruler (*Germanic*); diminutive forms are **Walburga, Walborga, Valburga**.

Valdemar *masc* a variant form of **Waldemar**.

Valdemaro *masc* an Italian form of **Waldemar**.

Valentin *masc* a French, German and Scandinavian form of **Valentine**.

Valentina *fem* form of **Valentine**; a diminutive form is **Val**.

Valentine *masc fem* strong; healthy; powerful (*Latin*); a diminutive form is **Val**.

Valentino *masc* an Italian form of **Valentine**.

Valerian *masc* form of **Valerie**.

Valeriano *masc* an Italian form of **Valerian**.

Valerie *fem* strong (*Latin*); a diminutive form is **Val**.

Valerio *masc* an Italian form of **Valerian**.

Valéry *masc* foreign power (*Germanic*).

Van *masc* from, of, a prefix in Dutch surnames now used independently as an English-language first name.

Vance *masc* young (*Old English*).

Vanessa *fem* a name invented by Jonathan Swift for his friend Esther Vanhomrigh, created from the prefix of her surname plus the suffix *essa*; a diminutive form is **Nessa**.

Vasili, Vassily *masc* Russian forms of **Basil**.

Vaughan, Vaughn *masc* a surname, meaning small one, used as a first name (*Welsh*).

Velvet *fem* the English name of a rich, soft cloth used as a first name .

Venetia *fem* the name of the region around Venice in northern Italy used as a first name (*Latin*).

Vera *fem* faith (*Russian*); true (*Latin*).

Vere *masc* a surname, meaning from Ver in France, used as a first name (*Old French*).

Vergil *masc* a variant form of **Virgil**.

Verity *fem* truth (*Latin*).

Verne, Verna *fem* diminutive forms of **Laverne**.

Vernon *masc* a surname, meaning alder tree, used as a first name (*Old French*).

Verona *fem* a variant form of **Veronica**.

Veronica *fem* true image (*Latin*); a variant form is **Verona**; diminutive forms are **Ronnie, Ronny**.

Veronika *fem* a Scandinavian form of **Veronica**.

Veronike *fem* a German form of **Veronica**.

Véronique *fem* a French form of **Veronica**.

Vesta *fem* of uncertain meaning; in Roman mythology, the goddess of the hearth (*Latin*).

Vi *fem* a diminutive form of **Viola, Violet**.

Vicente *masc* a Spanish form of **Vincent**.

Vicki, Vickie, Vicky *fem* a diminutive form of **Victoria**, now used independently.

Victoire *fem* a French form of **Victoria**.

Victor *masc* conqueror (*Latin*); a diminutive form is **Vic**.

Victoria *fem* victory (*Latin*); diminutive forms are **Tory, Vickie, Vita**.

Vidal *masc* a Spanish form of *vitalis* (*Latin*), living vital.

Vilhelm *masc* a Swedish form of **William**.

Vilhelmina *fem* a Swedish form of **Wilhelmina**.

Vilma *fem* a diminutive form of **Vilhelmina**.

Vincent *masc* conquering; victorious (*Latin*); diminutive forms are **Vince, Vinnie, Vinny**.

Vincente *masc* an Italian form of **Vincent**.

Vincentia *fem* form of **Vincent**.

Vincenz *masc* a German form of **Vincent**.

Vinnie, Vinny *masc* diminutive forms of **Vincent**.

Vinson *masc* a surname form of **Vincent** used as a first name (*Old English*).

Viola, Violet *fem* a violet (*Latin*); a diminutive form is **Vi**.

Violetta *fem* the Italian form of **Viola, Violet**.

Virgil *masc* staff bearer (*Latin*), the name of the Roman poet of the first century BC; a variant form is **Vergil**.

Virgilio *masc* the Italian and Spanish form of **Virgil**.

Virginia *fem* virginal (*Latin*); a diminutive form is **Ginnie**.

Virginie *fem* a Dutch and French form of **Virginia**.

Vita *fem* form of **Vito**; a diminutive form of **Victoria**.

Vitale *masc* an Italian form of *vitalis* (*Latin*), living, vital.

Vito *masc* the Italian form of **Vitus**.

Vitore *masc* an Italian form of **Victor**.

Vitoria *fem* a Spanish form of **Victoria**.

Vitorio *masc* the Spanish form of **Victor**.

Vittorio *masc* an Italian form of **Victor**.

Vitus *masc* life (*Latin*).

Viv *fem* a diminutive form of **Vivien**.

Vivian, Vyvian *masc* full of life (Latin); a variant form is **Vyvian**.

Vivien, Vivienne *fem* form of **Vivian**; a diminutive form is **Viv**.

Vladimir *masc* Royally famous. A renowned monarch (*Slavic*).

Vladislav *masc* great ruler (*Slavonic*).

Vyvian *masc* a variant form of **Vivian**.

W

Wade *masc* a surname, meaning to go, or at the ford, used as a first name (*Old English*).

Wadsworth *masc* a surname, meaning Wade's homestead, used as a first name (*Old English*); a variant form is **Wordsworth**.

Wainwright *masc* a surname, meaning maker of carts, used as a first name (*Old English*).

Wake *masc* a surname, meaning alert, watchful, used as a first name (*Old English*).

Waldo *masc* ruler (*Germanic*).

Waldemar *masc* noted ruler (*Germanic*); a variant form is **Valdemar**.

Walker *masc* a surname, meaning a fuller, used as a first name (*Old English*).

Wallace *masc* a Scots variant form of **Wallis**; a diminutive form is **Wally**.

Wallis *masc fem* a surname, meaning foreigner, used as a first name (*Old French*); a variant form is **Wallace**; a diminutive form is **Wally**.

Wally *masc* a diminutive form of **Wallace, Wallis**.

Walt masc a diminutive form of **Walter, Walton**.

Walter *masc* ruler of army, people (*Germanic*); diminutive forms are **Walt, Wat, Watty**.

Walther *masc* a German form of **Walter**.

Walton *masc* a surname, meaning farmstead of the Britons, used as a first name (*Old English*); a diminutive form is **Walt**.

Wanda *fem* a variant form of **Wenda**.

Ward *masc* a surname, meaning watchman; guard, used as a first name (*Old English*).

Warfield *masc* a surname, meaning field of the stream of the wrens, used as a first name (*Old English*).

Warne *masc* a surname, meaning alder wood, used as a first name (*Cornish*).

Warner *masc* a surname, meaning protecting army, used as a first name (*Germanic*).

Warren *masc* a surname, meaning wasteland or game park, used as a first name (*Old French*).

Warwick *masc* a placename and surname, meaning dwellings by the weir, used as a first name (*Old English*).

Washington *masc* a placename and surname, meaning Wassa's estate, used as a first name (*Old English*).

Wat, Watty *masc* a diminutive form of **Walter**.

Waverley *masc* a placename, meaning meadow or clearing by the swampy ground, used as a first name (*Old English*).

Wayne *masc* a surname, meaning a carter, used as a first name.

Webb *masc* a surname, meaning weaver, used as a first name (*Old English*).

Webster *masc* a surname, meaning woman weaver, used as a first name (*Old English*).

Wellington *masc* a placename and surname, meaning Weola's farmstead, used as a first name (*Old English*).

Wenceslaus, Wenceslas *masc* wreathed with glory (*Slavonic*).

Wenda *fem* form of **Wendel**; a variant form is **Wanda**.

Wendel, Wendell *masc* of the Wend people (*Germanic*); a variant form is **Wendel**.

Wendy *fem* invented by J. M. Barrie for the main female character in his play *Peter Pan*.

Wentworth *masc* a surname, meaning winter enclosure, used as a first name (*Old English*).

Werner *masc* a German form of **Warner**.

Wesley *masc* a surname, meaning west wood, made famous by the Methodists John and Charles Wesley, used as a first name (*Old English*); a diminutive form is **Wes**.

Whitaker *masc* a surname, meaning white acre, used as a first name (*Old English*); a variant form is **Whittaker**.

Whitman *masc* a surname, meaning white- or fair-haired, used as a first name (*Old English*).

Whitney *masc, fem* a surname and placename, meaning white island or Witta's island, used as a first name (*Old English*).

Whittaker *masc* a variant form of **Whitaker**.

Wilbert *masc* well-born (*Old English*).

Wilbur *masc* wild boar (*Old English*).

Wilfrida, Wilfreda *fem* form of **Wilfrid**.

Wilfrid, Wilfred *masc* will peace (*Germanic*); a diminutive form is **Wilf**.

Wilhelm *masc* the German form of **William**; a diminutive form is **Wim**.

Wilhelmina, Wilhelmine *fem* form of **Wilhelm**; diminutive forms are **Elma, Minna, Minnie, Wilma**.

Will, Willie, Willy *masc* diminutive forms of **William**.

Willa *fem* form of **Will, William**.

Willard *masc* a surname, meaning bold resolve, used as a first name (*Old English*).

Willemot *masc* resolute in spirit (*Germanic*).

William *masc* resolute helmet (Germanic); diminutive forms are Bill, Will.

Williamina *fem* form of **William**.

Willoughby *masc* a surname, meaning farm by the willows, used as a first name (*Old Norse/Old English*).

Willson *masc* a variant form of **Wilson**.

Wilma *fem* a diminutive form of **Wilhelmina**; *fem* form of **William**.

Wilmer *masc* famous will or desire (*Old English*);
  masc form of **Wilma**.

Wilmot *masc* a diminutive surname form of **William**
  used as a first name.

Wilson masc a surname, meaning son of Will, used as a
  first name (*Old English*); a variant form is **Willson**.

Wilton *masc* a placename and surname, meaning
  floodable place, used as a first name (*Old English*).

Wim *masc* a contraction of **Wilhelm**.

Windham *masc* a variant form of **Wyndham**.

Windsor *masc* a placename and surname, meaning
  slope with a windlass, used as a first name (*Old
  English*).

Winifred *fem* joy and peace (*Old English*); diminutive
  forms are **Freda, Win, Winnie, Wynn, Wynne**.

Winslow *masc* a placename and surname, meaning
  Wine's burial mound, used as a first name (*Old
  English*).

Winston *masc* a placename and surname, meaning
  friend's place or farm, used as a first name (*Old
  English*).

Winter *masc* the name for the cold season of the year
  used as a first name (*Old English*).

Winthrop *masc* a surname, meaning friend's farm
  village, used as a first name (*Old English*).

Winton *masc* a surname, meaning friend's farm, used
  as a first name (*Old English*).

Wolf, Wolfe *masc* wolf (*Old English*).

Wolfgang *masc* bold wolf (*Germanic*).

Wolfram *masc* wolf raven (*Germanic*).

Woodrow *masc* a surname, meaning row (of houses) in a wood, used as a first name; a diminutive form is **Woody**.

Woodward *masc* a surname, meaning forest guardian, used as a first name (*Old English*).

Woody *masc* a diminutive form of **Woodrow**, now used independently.

Wordsworth *masc* a variant form of **Wadsworth**.

Worth *masc* a surname, meaning farmstead, used as a first name (*Old English*).

Wyman *masc* a surname, meaning battle protector, used as a first name (*Old English*).

Wyn *masc* white (*Welsh*); a variant form is **Wynn**.

Wyndham *masc* a surname, meaning homestead of Wyman, used as a first name (*Old English*); a variant form is **Windham**.

Wynn, Wynne *masc, fem* a surname, meaning friend, used as a first name; *masc* a variant form of **Wyn**; *fem* a diminutive form of **Winifred**.

X

Xanthe *fem* yellow (*Greek*).

Xavier *masc* a placename, meaning new house owner, used as a first name (*Spanish/Basque*).

Xaviera *fem* form of **Xavier**.

Xena, Xene, Xenia *fem* hospitality (*Greek*).

Xenos *masc* stranger (*Greek*).

Xerxes *masc* royal (*Persian*).

Y

Yale *masc* a surname, meaning fertile upland (*Welsh*).

Yasmin, Yasmine *fem* variant forms of **Jasmine**.

Yehuda *fem* a variant form of **Jehuda**.

Yehudi *masc* a Jew (*Hebrew*).

Yolanda, Yolande *fem* a variant form of **Viola**.

York, Yorke *masc* a placename and surname, meaning estate of Eburos or of the yew trees, used as a first name (*Celtic/Latin/Old English*).

Yseult *fem* an old French form of **Isolde**.

Yuri *masc* a Russian form of **George**.

Yves *masc* yew tree (*French-Germanic*).

Yvette *fem* a diminutive form of Yves.

Yvonne *fem* form of **Yves**.

Z

Zabdiel *masc* gift of God (*Hebrew*).

Zabrina *fem* a variant form of **Sabrina**.

Zaccheus *masc* innocent; pure (*Hebrew*).

Zachary, Zachariah, Zacharias, Zecheriah*masc* Jehovah has remembered (*Hebrew*); diminutive forms are **Zach, Zack, Zak**.

Zadok *masc* righteous (*Hebrew*).

Zara *fem* flower (*Arabic*).

Zeb *masc* a diminutive form of **Zebadiah, Zebedee, Zebulun**.

Zebadiah, Zebedee *masc* gift of the Lord (*Hebrew*).

Zebulon, Zebulun *masc* elevation (*Hebrew*); diminutive forms are **Lonny, Zeb**.

Zedekiah *masc* justice of the Lord (*Hebrew*); a diminutive form is **Zed**.

Zeke *masc* a diminutive form of **Ezekiel**.

Zelig *masc* a variant form of **Selig**.

Zelma *fem* a variant form of **Selma**.

Zenas *masc* gift of Zeus (*Greek*).

Zenobia *fem* having life from Zeus (*Greek*).

Zephaniah *masc* hid of the Lord (*Hebrew*); a diminutive form is **Zeph**.

Zinnia *fem* the name of a plant with brightly coloured flowers used as a first name, named after the German botanist J. G. Zinn.

Zoë, Zoe *fem* life (*Greek*).